----

12 Tribes

Israelite Precepts

By Jahkim Ben Israel

BLACKSTONE PUBLISHING

Orlando, FL June 2024

12 Tribes Of Israel

Judah - American Blacks

Benjamin - West Indian Blacks

Levi - Haitians

Ephraim - Puerto Ricans

Manasseh - Cubans

Simeon - Dominicans

Zebulon - Guatemala to Panama (Mayans)

Gad - Native-American Indians

Reuben - Seminole Indians

Asher - Columbia to Uruguay (Incas)

Issachar - Mexicans (Aztecs)

Naphtali - Argentina/Chile

Table of Contents

The Color of Israelites...........4
Black Like Egyptians............5
Israel in Slavery..................8
Esau...............................16
Migration of The
10 Tribes of Israel..............18
Israel in Americas..............19
What is Love.....................20
The Holy Ghost.................20
The Church in Israel...........20
New Testament Only for
Israel..............................21
First Born= Heir................22
Saints.............................22
God Loves Israel...............23
Salvation for Israel............24
World.............................25
Whoesoever......................26
He Foreknew....................27
Elect..............................27
Chosen............................28
Islam created in 622 AD.......29
Immaculate Conception
Lie.................................30
Marriage..........................33
Divorce...........................36
Good Wife.......................37

Evil Women.....................38
Order of Women...............40
Marriage Sex Laws...........41
Christmas........................45
Study.............................46
Study the Whole Bible.......46
The Bible is Only For
Israel..............................47
How to Read the Bible.......47
Oppression......................48
Israelites Called Heathens...49
Israelites Called Gentiles...49
Real Gentile Nations.........50
Stranger Nations..............51
Israel Called Strangers.......53
Interracial Marriage..........54
Regeneration...................55
UFO's Are Chariots..........57
Sabbath..........................58
Dress Code......................59
Hatred............................60
Destruction......................61
Nations in Captivity..........63
Baptism..........................66
Solutions........................66
High Holy Days...............68

The Color of Israelites

❖ **Gen.2:7** And the LORD God formed man *of* the dust of the ground, and breathed into his nostrils the breath of life; and man became a living soul.

❖ **Jer.14:2** Judah mourneth, and the gates thereof languish; they are black unto the ground; and the cry of Jerusalem is gone up.

   Job.30:30 My skin is black upon me, and my bones are burned with heat.

❖ **Song of Sol.1:5** I *am* dark, but lovely, O daughters of Jerusalem, Like the tents of Kedar, Like the curtains of Solomon.

❖ **Lamentations 4:7-8** Her Nazirites were brighter than snow And whiter than milk; They were more ruddy in body than rubies, *Like* sapphire in their appearance. *Now* their appearance is blacker than soot; They go unrecognized in the streets; Their skin clings to their bones, It has become as dry as wood.

❖ **Lamentations 5:10** Our skin was black like an oven because of the terrible famine.

❖ **Jeremiah 8:21** For the hurt of the daughter of my people am I hurt; I am black; astonishment hath taken hold on me.

Black like Egyptians

❖ **Genesis 42:7-8:23** 7 And Joseph saw his brethren, and he knew them, but made himself strange unto them, and spake roughly unto them; and he said unto them, Whence come ye? And they said, From the land of Canaan to buy food. [8] And Joseph knew his brethren, but they knew not him. [9] And Joseph remembered the dreams which he dreamed of them, and said unto them, Ye are spies; to see the nakedness of the land ye are come. [10] And they said unto him, Nay, my lord, but to buy food are thy servants come. [11] We are all one man's sons; we are true men, thy servants are no spies. [12] And he said unto them, Nay, but to see the nakedness of the land ye are come. [13] And they said, Thy servants are twelve brethren, the sons of one man in the land of Canaan; and, behold, the youngest is this day with our father, and one is not. [14] And Joseph said unto them, That is it that I spake unto you, saying, Ye are spies: [15] Hereby ye shall be proved: By the life of Pharaoh ye shall not go forth hence, except your youngest brother come hither. [16] Send one of you, and let him fetch your brother, and ye shall be kept in prison, that your words may be proved, whether there be any truth in you: or else by the life of Pharaoh surely ye are spies. [17] And he put them all together into ward three days. [18] And Joseph said unto them the third day, This do, and live; for I fear God: [19] If ye be true men, let one of your brethren be bound in the house of your prison: go ye, carry corn for the famine of your houses: [20] But bring your youngest brother unto me; so shall your words be verified, and ye shall not die. And they did so. [21] And they said one to another, We are verily guilty concerning our brother, in that we saw the anguish of his soul, when he besought us, and we would not hear; therefore is this distress come upon us. ²² And Reuben answered them, saying, Spake I not unto you, saying, Do not sin against the child; and ye would not hear? therefore, behold, also his blood is required. ²³ And they knew not that Joseph understood them; for he spake unto them by an interpreter. ²⁴ And he turned himself about from them, and wept; and returned to them again, and communed with them, and took from them Simeon, and bound him before their eyes. ²⁵ Then Joseph commanded to fill their sacks with corn, and to restore every man's money into his sack, and to give them provision for the way: and thus did he unto them. ²⁶ And they laded their asses with the corn, and departed thence. ²⁷ And as one of them opened his sack to give his ass provender in the inn, he espied his money; for, behold, it was in his sack's mouth. ²⁸ And he said unto his brethren, My money is restored; and, lo, it is even in my sack: and their heart failed them, and they were afraid, saying one to another, What is this that God hath done unto us? ²⁹ And they came unto Jacob their father unto the land of Canaan, and told him all that befell unto them; saying, ³⁰ The man, who is the lord of the land, spake roughly to us, and took us for spies of the country. ³¹ And we said unto him, We are true men; we are no spies: ³² We be twelve brethren, sons of our father; one is not, and the youngest is this day with our father in the land of Canaan. ³³ And the man, the lord of the country, said unto us, Hereby shall I know that ye are true men; leave one of your brethren here with me, and take food for the famine of your households, and be gone: ³⁴ And bring your youngest brother unto me: then shall I know that ye are no spies, but that ye are true men: so will I deliver you your brother, and ye shall traffick in the land. ³⁵ And it came to pass as they emptied their sacks, that, behold, every man's bundle of money was in his sack: and when both they and their father saw the bundles of money, they were afraid. ³⁶ And Jacob their father said unto them, Me have ye bereaved of my children: Joseph is not, and Simeon is not, and ye will

take Benjamin away: all these things are against me.
[37] And Reuben spake unto his father, saying, Slay my two sons, if I bring him not to thee: deliver him into my hand, and I will bring him to thee again. [38] And he said, My son shall not go down with you; for his brother is dead, and he is left alone: if mischief befall him by the way in the which ye go, then shall ye bring down my gray hairs with sorrow to the grave.

❖ **Exodus 2:19** And they said, An Egyptian delivered us out of the hand of the shepherds, and also drew *water* enough for us, and watered the flock.

❖ **Acts.21:37-39** And as Paul was to be led into the castle, he said unto the chief captain, May I speak unto thee? Who said, Canst thou speak Greek? Art not thou that Egyptian, which before these days madest an uproar, and leddest out into the wilderness four thousand men that were murderers? But Paul said, I am a man *which am* a Jew of Tarsus, *a city* in Cilicia, a citizen of no mean city: and, I beseech thee, suffer me to speak unto the people.

❖ **Exodus 4:6-7** And the LORD said furthermore unto him, Put now thine hand into thy bosom. And he put his hand into his bosom: and when he took it out, behold, his hand *was* leprous as snow. And he said, Put thine hand into thy bosom again. And he put his hand into his bosom again; and plucked it out of his bosom, and, behold, it was turned again as his *other* flesh.

❖ **Numbers 12:9-12** And the anger of the LORD was kindled against them; and he departed. And the cloud departed from off the tabernacle; and, behold, Miriam *became* leprous, *white* as snow: and Aaron looked upon Miriam, and, behold, *she was* leprous. And Aaron said unto Moses, Alas, my lord, I beseech thee, lay not the sin upon us, wherein we have done foolishly, and wherein we have sinned. Let her not be as one dead, of whom the flesh is half consumed when he cometh out of his mother's womb.

❖ **Daniel 10:5-6** Then I lifted up mine eyes, and looked, and behold a certain man clothed in linen, whose loins *were* girded with fine gold of Uphaz: His body also *was* like the beryl, and his face as the appearance of lightning, and his eyes as lamps of fire, and his arms and his feet like in colour to polished brass, and the voice of his words like the voice of a multitude.

❖ **Revelation 1:14-15** His head and *his* hairs *were* white like wool, as white as snow; and his eyes *were* as a flame of fire; And his feet like unto fine brass, as if they burned in a furnace; and his voice as the sound of many waters.

ISRAEL IN SLAVERY

❖ **Deuteronomy 28:15-68** But it shall come to pass, if you will not hearken unto the voice of the LORD your God, to observe to do all his commandments and his statutes which I command you this day; that all these curses shall come upon you, and overtake you: Cursed *shalt* thou *be* in the city, and cursed *shalt* thou *be* in the field. Cursed *shall be* thy basket and thy store. Cursed *shall be* the fruit of thy body, and the fruit of thy land, the increase of thy kine, and the flocks of thy sheep. Cursed *shalt* thou *be* when thou comest in, and cursed *shalt* thou *be* when thou goest out. But it shall come to pass, if thou wilt not hearken unto the voice of the LORD thy God, to observe to do all his commandments and his statutes which I command thee this day; that all these curses shall come upon thee, and overtake thee: [16] Cursed shalt thou be in the city, and cursed shalt thou be in the field. [17] Cursed shall be thy basket and thy store. [18] Cursed shall be the fruit of thy body, and the fruit of thy land, the increase of thy kine, and the flocks of thy sheep. [19] Cursed shalt thou be when thou comest in, and cursed shalt thou be when thou goest out. [20] The LORD shall send upon thee cursing, vexation, and rebuke, in all that thou settest thine hand unto for to do, until thou be destroyed, and until thou perish quickly; because of the wickedness of thy doings, whereby thou hast forsaken me. [21] The LORD shall make the pestilence cleave unto thee, until he have consumed thee from off the land, whither thou goest to possess it. [22] The LORD shall smite thee with a consumption, and with a fever, and with an inflammation, and with an extreme burning, and with the sword, and with blasting, and with mildew; and they shall pursue thee until thou perish. [23] And thy heaven that is over thy head shall be brass, and the earth that is under thee shall be iron. [24] The LORD shall make the rain of thy land powder and dust: from heaven shall it come down upon thee, until thou be destroyed. [25] The LORD shall cause thee to be smitten before thine enemies: thou shalt go out one way against them, and flee seven ways before them: and shalt be removed into all the kingdoms of the earth. [26] And thy carcase shall be meat unto all fowls of the air, and unto the beasts of the earth, and no man shall fray them away. [27] The LORD will smite thee with the botch of Egypt, and with the emerods, and with the scab, and with the itch, whereof thou canst not be healed. [28] The LORD shall smite thee with madness, and blindness, and astonishment of heart: [29] And thou shalt grope at noonday, as the blind gropeth in darkness, and thou shalt not prosper in thy ways: and thou shalt be only oppressed and spoiled evermore, and no man shall save thee. [30] Thou shalt betroth a wife, and another man shall lie with her: thou shalt build an house, and thou shalt not dwell therein: thou shalt plant a vineyard, and shalt not gather the grapes thereof. [31] Thine ox shall be slain before thine eyes, and thou shalt not eat thereof: thine ass shall be violently taken away from before thy face, and shall not be restored to thee: thy sheep shall be given unto thine enemies, and thou shalt have none to rescue them. ³² Thy sons and thy daughters shall be given unto another people, and thine eyes shall look, and fail with longing for them all the day long; and there shall be no might in thine hand. ³³ The fruit of thy land, and all thy labours, shall a nation which thou knowest not eat up; and thou shalt be only oppressed and crushed alway: ³⁴ So that thou shalt be mad for the sight of thine eyes which thou shalt see. ³⁵ The LORD shall smite thee in the knees, and in the legs, with a sore botch that cannot be healed, from the sole of thy foot unto the top of thy head. ³⁶ The LORD shall bring thee, and thy king which thou shalt set over thee, unto a nation which neither thou nor thy fathers have known; and there shalt thou serve other gods, wood and stone. ³⁷ And thou shalt become an astonishment, a proverb, and a byword, among all nations whither the LORD shall lead thee. ³⁸ Thou shalt carry much seed out into the field, and shalt gather but little in; for the locust shall consume it. ³⁹ Thou shalt plant vineyards, and dress them, but shalt neither drink of the wine, nor gather the grapes; for the worms shall eat them. ⁴⁰ Thou shalt have olive trees throughout all thy coasts, but thou shalt not anoint thyself with the oil; for thine olive shall cast his fruit. ⁴¹ Thou shalt beget sons and daughters, but thou shalt not enjoy them; for they shall go into captivity. ⁴² All thy trees and fruit of thy land shall the locust consume. ⁴³ The stranger that is within thee shall get up above thee very high; and thou shalt come down very low. ⁴⁴ He shall lend to thee, and thou shalt not lend to him: he shall be the head, and thou shalt be the tail. ⁴⁵ Moreover all these curses shall come upon thee, and shall pursue thee, and overtake thee, till thou be destroyed; because thou hearkenedst not unto the voice of the LORD thy God, to keep his commandments and his statutes which he commanded thee: ⁴⁶ And they shall be upon thee for a sign and for a wonder, and upon thy seed for ever. ⁴⁷ Because thou servedst not the LORD thy God with joyfulness, and with gladness of heart, for the abundance of all things; ⁴⁸ Therefore shalt thou serve thine enemies which the LORD shall send against thee, in hunger, and in thirst, and in nakedness, and in want of all things: and he shall put a yoke of iron upon thy neck, until he have destroyed thee. ⁴⁹ The LORD shall bring a nation against thee from far, from the end of the earth, as swift as the eagle flieth; a nation whose tongue thou shalt not understand; ⁵⁰ A nation of fierce countenance, which shall not regard the person of the old, nor shew favour to the young: ⁵¹ And he shall eat the fruit of thy cattle, and the fruit of thy land, until thou be destroyed: which also shall not leave thee either corn, wine, or oil, or the increase of thy kine, or flocks of thy sheep, until he have destroyed thee. ⁵² And he shall besiege thee in all thy gates, until thy high and fenced walls come down, wherein thou trustedst, throughout all thy land: and he shall besiege thee in all thy gates throughout all thy land, which the LORD thy God hath given thee. ⁵³ And thou shalt eat the fruit of thine own body, the flesh of thy sons and of thy daughters, which the LORD thy God hath given thee, in the siege, and in the straitness, wherewith thine enemies shall distress thee: ⁵⁴ So that the man that is tender among you, and very delicate, his eye shall be evil toward his brother, and toward the wife of his bosom, and toward the remnant of his children which he shall leave: ⁵⁵ So that he will not give to any of them of the flesh of his children whom he shall eat: because he hath nothing left him in the siege, and in the straitness, wherewith thine enemies shall distress thee in all thy gates. ⁵⁶ The tender and delicate woman among you, which would not adventure to set the sole of her foot upon the ground for delicateness and tenderness, her eye shall be evil toward the husband of her bosom, and toward her son, and toward her daughter, ⁵⁷ And toward her young one that cometh out from between her feet, and toward her children which she shall bear: for she shall eat them for want of all things secretly in the siege and straitness, wherewith thine enemy shall distress thee in thy gates. ⁵⁸ If thou wilt not observe to do all the words of this law that are written in this book, that thou mayest fear this glorious and fearful name, THE LORD THY GOD; [59] Then the LORD will make thy plagues wonderful, and the plagues of thy seed, even great plagues, and of long continuance, and sore sicknesses, and of long continuance. [60] Moreover he will bring upon thee all the diseases of Egypt, which thou wast afraid of; and they shall cleave unto thee. [61] Also every sickness, and every plague, which is not written in the book of this law, them will the LORD bring upon thee, until thou be destroyed. [62] And ye shall be left few in number, whereas ye were as the stars of heaven for multitude; because thou wouldest not obey the voice of the LORD thy God. [63] And it shall come to pass, that as the LORD rejoiced over you to do you good, and to multiply you; so the LORD will rejoice over you to destroy you, and to bring you to nought; and ye shall be plucked from off the land whither thou goest to possess it. [64] And the LORD shall scatter thee among all people, from the one end of the earth even unto the other; and there thou shalt serve other gods, which neither thou nor thy fathers have known, even wood and stone. [65] And among these nations shalt thou find no ease, neither shall the sole of thy foot have rest: but the LORD shall give thee there a trembling heart, and failing of eyes, and sorrow of mind: [66] And thy life shall hang in doubt before thee; and thou shalt fear day and night, and shalt have none assurance of thy life: [67] In the morning thou shalt say, Would God it were even! and at even thou shalt say, Would God it were morning! for the fear of thine heart wherewith thou shalt fear, and for the sight of thine eyes which thou shalt see. [68] And the LORD shall bring thee into Egypt again with ships, by the way whereof I spake unto thee, Thou shalt see it no more again: and there ye shall be sold unto your enemies for bondmen and bondwomen, and no man shall buy you.

❖ **Leviticus 26:14-46** [14] But if ye will not hearken unto me, and will not do all these commandments; [15] And if ye shall

12

despise my statutes, or if your soul abhor my judgments, so that ye will not do all my commandments, but that ye break my covenant: [16] I also will do this unto you; I will even appoint over you terror, consumption, and the burning ague, that shall consume the eyes, and cause sorrow of heart: and ye shall sow your seed in vain, for your enemies shall eat it. [17] And I will set my face against you, and ye shall be slain before your enemies: they that hate you shall reign over you; and ye shall flee when none pursueth you. [18] And if ye will not yet for all this hearken unto me, then I will punish you seven times more for your sins. [19] And I will break the pride of your power; and I will make your heaven as iron, and your earth as brass: [20] And your strength shall be spent in vain: for your land shall not yield her increase, neither shall the trees of the land yield their fruits. [21] And if ye walk contrary unto me, and will not hearken unto me; I will bring seven times more plagues upon you according to your sins. [22] I will also send wild beasts among you, which shall rob you of your children, and destroy your cattle, and make you few in number; and your high ways shall be desolate. [23] And if ye will not be reformed by me by these things, but will walk contrary unto me; [24] Then will I also walk contrary unto you, and will punish you yet seven times for your sins. [25] And I will bring a sword upon you, that shall avenge the quarrel of my covenant: and when ye are gathered together within your cities, I will send the pestilence among you; and ye shall be delivered into the hand of the enemy. [26] And when I have broken the staff of your bread, ten women shall bake your bread in one oven, and they shall deliver you your bread again by weight: and ye shall eat, and not be satisfied. [27] And if ye will not for all this hearken unto me, but walk contrary unto me; [28] Then I will walk contrary unto you also in fury; and I, even I, will chastise you seven times for your sins. [29] And ye shall eat the flesh of your sons, and the flesh of your daughters shall ye eat. [30] And I will destroy your high places, and cut down your images, and cast your carcases upon the carcases of your idols, and my soul shall abhor you. [31] And I will make your cities waste, and bring your sanctuaries unto desolation, and I will not smell the savour of your sweet odours. [32] And I will bring the land into desolation: and your enemies which dwell therein shall be astonished at it. [33] And I will scatter you among the heathen, and will draw out a sword after you: and your land shall be desolate, and your cities waste. [34] Then shall the land enjoy her sabbaths, as long as it lieth desolate, and ye be in your enemies' land; even then shall the land rest, and enjoy her sabbaths. [35] As long as it lieth desolate it shall rest; because it did not rest in your sabbaths, when ye dwelt upon it. [36] And upon them that are left alive of you I will send a faintness into their hearts in the lands of their enemies; and the sound of a shaken leaf shall chase them; and they shall flee, as fleeing from a sword; and they shall fall when none pursueth. [37] And they shall fall one upon another, as it were before a sword, when none pursueth: and ye shall have no power to stand before your enemies. [38] And ye shall perish among the heathen, and the land of your enemies shall eat you up. [39] And they that are left of you shall pine away in their iniquity in your enemies' lands; and also in the iniquities of their fathers shall they pine away with them. [40] If they shall confess their iniquity, and the iniquity of their fathers, with their trespass which they trespassed against me, and that also they have walked contrary unto me; [41] And that I also have walked contrary unto them, and have brought them into the land of their enemies; if then their uncircumcised hearts be humbled, and they then accept of the punishment of their iniquity: [42] Then will I remember my covenant with Jacob, and also my covenant with Isaac, and also my covenant with Abraham will I remember; and I will remember the land. [43] The land also shall be left of them, and shall enjoy her sabbaths, while she lieth desolate without them: and they shall accept of the punishment of their iniquity: because, even because they despised my judgments, and because their soul abhorred my statutes. [44] And yet for all that, when they be in the land of their enemies, I will not cast them away, neither will I abhor them, to destroy them utterly, and to break my covenant with them: for I am the LORD their God. ⁴⁵ But I will for their sakes remember the covenant of their ancestors, whom I brought forth out of the land of Egypt in the sight of the heathen, that I might be their God: I am the LORD. ⁴⁶ These are the statutes and judgments and laws, which the LORD made between him and the children of Israel in mount Sinai by the hand of Moses.

❖ **1 Kings 8:44-47** ⁴⁴ If thy people go out to battle against their enemy, whithersoever thou shalt send them, and shall pray unto the LORD toward the city which thou hast chosen, and toward the house that I have built for thy name: ⁴⁵ Then hear thou in heaven their prayer and their supplication, and maintain their cause. ⁴⁶ If they sin against thee, (for there is no man that sinneth not,) and thou be angry with them, and deliver them to the enemy, so that they carry them away captives unto the land of the enemy, far or near; ⁴⁷ Yet if they shall bethink themselves in the land whither they were carried captives, and repent, and make supplication unto thee in the land of them that carried them captives, saying, We have sinned, and have done perversely, we have committed wickedness;

❖ **Joel 3:1-6** 3 For, behold, in those days, and in that time, when I shall bring again the captivity of Judah and Jerusalem, ² I will also gather all nations, and will bring them down into the valley of Jehoshaphat, and will plead with them there for my people and for my heritage Israel, whom they have scattered among the nations, and parted my land. ³ And they have cast lots for my people; and have given a boy for an harlot, and sold a girl for wine, that they might drink. ⁴ Yea, and what have ye to do with me, O

Tyre, and Zidon, and all the coasts of Palestine? will ye render me a recompence? and if ye recompense me, swiftly and speedily will I return your recompence upon your own head; ⁵ Because ye have taken my silver and my gold, and have carried into your temples my goodly pleasant things: ⁶ The children also of Judah and the children of Jerusalem have ye sold unto the Grecians, that ye might remove them far from their border.

❖ **Luke 21:20-24** ²⁰ And when ye shall see Jerusalem compassed with armies, then know that the desolation thereof is nigh. ²¹ Then let them which are in Judaea flee to the mountains; and let them which are in the midst of it depart out; and let not them that are in the countries enter thereinto. ²² For these be the days of vengeance, that all things which are written may be fulfilled. ²³ But woe unto them that are with child, and to them that give suck, in those days! for there shall be great distress in the land, and wrath upon this people. ²⁴ And they shall fall by the edge of the sword, and shall be led away captive into all nations: and Jerusalem shall be trodden down of the Gentiles, until the times of the Gentiles be fulfilled.

❖ **Jeremiah 22:13** Woe unto him that buildeth his house by unrighteousness, and his chambers by wrong; *that* useth his neighbour's service without wages, and giveth him not for his work.

Esau

❖ **Genesis 25:21-25, 30** 21 And Isaac intreated the LORD for his wife, because she was barren: and the LORD was intreated of him, and Rebekah his wife conceived. 22 And the children struggled together within her; and she said, If it be so, why am I thus? And she went to enquire of the

LORD. 23 And the LORD said unto her, Two nations are in thy womb, and two manner of people shall be separated from thy bowels; and the one people shall be stronger than the other people; and the elder shall serve the younger. 24 And when her days to be delivered were fulfilled, behold, there were twins in her womb. 25 And the first came out red, all over like an hairy garment; and they called his name Esau. 30 And Esau said to Jacob, Feed me, I pray thee, with that same red pottage; for I am faint: therefore was his name called Edom.

❖ **Genesis 27: 38-40** 38 Esau said to his father, "Do you have only one blessing, my father? Bless me too, my father!" Then Esau wept aloud. 39 His father Isaac answered him, "Your dwelling will be away from the earth's richness, away from the dew of heaven above. 40 You will live by the sword and you will serve your brother. But when you grow restless, you will throw his yoke from off your neck."

❖ **Obadiah 1: 1 -4** 1 The vision of Obadiah. This is what the Sovereign LORD says about Edom. We have heard a message from the LORD: An envoy was sent to the nations to say, "Rise, let us go against her for battle" 2 "See, I will make you small among the nations; you will be utterly despised. 3 The pride of your heart has deceived you, you who live in the clefts of the rocks and make your home on the heights, you who say to yourself, 'Who can bring me down to the ground?' 4 Though you soar like the eagle and make your nest among the stars, from there I will bring you down," declares the LORD.

❖ **Malachi 1: 2 -4** 2 I have loved you, saith the LORD. Yet ye say, Wherein hast thou loved us? Was not Esau Jacob's brother? saith the LORD: yet I loved Jacob, 3 And I hated Esau, and laid his mountains and his heritage waste for the dragons of the wilderness. 4 Whereas Edom saith, We are impoverished, but we will return and build the desolate places; thus saith the LORD of hosts, They shall build, but I will throw down; and they shall call them, The border of wickedness, and, The people against whom the LORD hath indignation for ever.

❖ **Job 9:24 24** The earth is given into the hand of the wicked: he covereth the faces of the judges thereof; if not, where, and who is he?

❖ **2 Esdras 6: 8 -9** 8 And he said unto me, From Abraham unto Isaac, when Jacob and Esau were born of him, Jacob's hand held first the heel of Esau. 9 For Esau is the end of the world, and Jacob is the beginning of it that followeth.

<u>Migration of The 10 Tribes of Israel (Northern Kingdom)</u>

❖ **2 Esdras 13:40-45** 40 Those are the ten tribes, which were carried away prisoners out of their own land in the time of Osea the king, whom Salmanasar the king of Assyria led away captive, and he carried them over the waters, and so came they into another land. 41 But they took this counsel among themselves, that they would leave the multitude of the heathen, and go forth into a further country, where never mankind dwelt, 42 That they might there keep their statutes, which they never kept in their own land. 43 And they entered into Euphrates by the narrow places of the river. 44 For the most High then shewed signs for them, and held still the flood, till they were passed over. 45 For through that country there was a great way to go, namely, of a year and a half: and the same region is called Arsareth.

18

- ❖ **Deuteronomy 33:17** 17 His glory is like the firstling of his bullock, and his horns are like the horns of unicorns: with them he shall push the people together to the ends of the earth: and they are the ten thousands of Ephraim, and they are the thousands of Manasseh.

- ❖ **Hosea 11: 10** 10 They shall walk after the Lord: he shall roar like a lion: when he shall roar, then the children shall tremble from the west.

ISRAEL IN AMERICAS

- ❖ **Jeremiah 16:14-15** 14 Therefore, behold, the days come, saith the Lord, that it shall no more be said, The Lord liveth, that brought up the children of Israel out of the land of Egypt; 15 But, The Lord liveth, that brought up the children of Israel from the land of the north, and from all the lands whither he had driven them: and I will bring them again into their land that I gave unto their fathers.

- ❖ **Isaiah 14:13** 13 For thou hast said in thine heart, I will ascend into heaven, I will exalt my throne above the stars of God: I will sit also upon the mount of the congregation, in the sides of the north:

- ❖ **Revelation 18:4** And I heard another voice from heaven, saying, Come out of her, my people, that ye be not partakers of her sins, and that ye receive not of her plagues.

WHAT IS LOVE?

❖ **John 14:15** If ye love me, keep my commandments.

❖ **1 John 5:3** For this is the love of God, that we keep his commandments: and his commandments are not grievous.

❖ **2 John 6** And this is love, that we walk after his commandments. This is the commandment, That, as ye have heard from the beginning, ye should walk in it.

❖ **Romans 13:10** Love worketh no ill to his neighbour: therefore love is the fulfilling of the law.

❖ **Wisdom Of Solomon 6:18** And love is the keeping of her laws; and the giving heed unto her laws is the assurance of incorruption;

❖ **Ecclesiasticus 2:15** "They that fear the Lord will not disobey his Word; and they that love him will keep his ways."

The Holy Ghost

❖ **Acts 7:51-53** 51 Ye stiffnecked and uncircumcised in heart and ears, ye do always resist the Holy Ghost: as your fathers [did], so [do] ye. 52 Which of the prophets have not your fathers persecuted? and they have slain them which shewed before of the coming of the Just One; of whom ye have been now the betrayers and murderers: 53 Who have received the law by the disposition of angels, and have not kept [it].

The Church is Israel

❖ **Acts 7:37-38** 37 This is that Moses, which said unto the children of Israel, A prophet shall the Lord your God raise up unto you of your brethren, like unto me; him shall ye hear. 38 This is he, that was in the church in the wilderness with the angel which spake to him in the mount Sina, and [with] our fathers: who received the lively oracles to give unto us:

❖ **Hebrews 12:23** To the general assembly and church of the firstborn, which are written in heaven, and to God the Judge of all, and to the spirits of just men made perfect

NEW TESTAMENT ONLY FOR ISRAEL

❖ **Hebrews 8:8-10** 8 For finding fault with them, he saith, Behold, the days come, saith the Lord, when I will make a new covenant with the house of Israel and with the house of Judah: 9 Not according to the covenant that I made with their fathers in the day when I took them by the hand to lead them out of the land of Egypt; because they continued not in my covenant, and I regarded them not, saith the Lord. 10 For this [is] the covenant that I will make with the house of Israel after those days, saith the Lord; I will put my laws into their mind, and write them in their hearts: and I will be to them a God, and they shall be to me a people

❖ **Jeremiah 31:31-33** 31 Behold, the days come, saith the LORD, that I will make a new covenant with the house of Israel, and with the house of Judah: 32 Not according to the covenant that I made with their fathers in the day [that] I took them by the hand to bring them out of the land of Egypt; which my covenant they brake, although I was an husband unto them, saith the LORD: 33 But this [shall be] the covenant that I will make with the house of Israel; After those days, saith the LORD, I will put my law in their inward parts, and write it in their hearts; and will be their God, and they shall be my people.

- ❖ **Romans 9:4** Who are Israelites; to whom pertaineth the adoption, and the glory, and the covenants, and the giving of the law, and the service of God, and the promises

- ❖ **Psalms 147:19-20** 19 He sheweth his word unto Jacob, his statutes and his judgments unto Israel. 20 He hath not dealt so with any nation: and [as for his] judgments, they have not known them. Praise ye the LORD.

Firstborn = Heir

- ❖ **Exodus 4:22** 22 And thou shalt say unto Pharaoh, Thus saith the Lord, Israel is my son, even my firstborn

- ❖ **Hebrews 12:23** 23 To the general assembly and church of the firstborn, which are written in heaven, and to God the Judge of all, and to the spirits of just men made perfect

- ❖ **2 Edsras 6:58-59** 58 But we thy people, whom thou hast called thy firstborn, thy only begotten, and thy fervent lover, are given into their hands. 59 If the world now be made for our sakes, why do we not possess an inheritance with the world? how long shall this endure?

- ❖ **Romans 8:16-17** 16 The Spirit itself beareth witness with our spirit, that we are the children of God: 17 And if children, then heirs; heirs of God, and joint-heirs with Christ; if so be that we suffer with [him], that we may be also glorified together.

SAINTS

- ❖ **Psalms 148:14** He also exalteth the horn of his people, the praise of all his saints; even of the children of Israel, a people near unto him. Praise ye the LORD.

- ❖ **Psalms 50:5** Gather my saints together unto me; those that have made a covenant with me by sacrifice.

- ❖ **Daniel 7:27** And the kingdom and dominion, and the greatness of the kingdom under the whole heaven, shall be given to the people of the saints of the most High, whose kingdom is an everlasting kingdom, and all dominions shall serve and obey him.

- ❖ **1 Corinthians 1:1- 2** 1 Paul, called [to be] an apostle of Jesus Christ through the will of God, and Sosthenes [our] brother, 2 Unto the church of God which is at Corinth, to them that are sanctified in Christ Jesus, called [to be] saints, with all that in every place call upon the name of Jesus Christ our Lord, both theirs and ours

- ❖ **Ephesians 1:1** Paul, an apostle of Jesus Christ by the will of God, to the saints which are at Ephesus, and to the faithful in Christ Jesus

- ❖ **Romans 1:7** To all that be in Rome, beloved of God, called to be saints: Grace to you and peace from God our Father, and the Lord Jesus Christ.

<u>GOD LOVES ISRAEL</u>

- ❖ **2 chronicles 9:8** Blessed be the LORD thy God, which delighted in thee to set thee on his throne, to be king for the LORD thy God: because thy God loved Israel, to establish them for ever, therefore made he thee king over them, to do judgment and justice.

- ❖ **Hosea 11:1** When Israel was a child, then I loved him, and called my son out of Egypt.

- ❖ **Psalms 47:4** He shall choose our inheritance for us, the excellency of Jacob whom he loved. Selah.

- ❖ **Malachi 1:2** I have loved you, saith the LORD. Yet ye say, Wherein hast thou loved us? Was not Esau Jacob's brother? saith the LORD: yet I loved Jacob

- ❖ **Romans 9:13** As it is written, Jacob have I loved, but Esau have I hated.

- ❖ **Deuteronomy 7:8** But because the LORD loved you, and because he would keep the oath which he had sworn unto your fathers, hath the LORD brought you out with a mighty hand, and redeemed you out of the house of bondmen, from the hand of Pharaoh king of Egypt.

SALVATION FOR ISRAEL

- ❖ **Daniel 12:1** And at that time shall Michael stand up, the great prince which standeth for the children of thy people: and there shall be a time of trouble, such as never was since there was a nation even to that same time: and at that time thy people shall be delivered, every one that shall be found written in the book.

- ❖ **Isaiah 45:17** But Israel shall be saved in the LORD with an everlasting salvation: ye shall not be ashamed nor confounded world without end.

- ❖ **Jeremiah 23:6** In his days Judah shall be saved, and Israel shall dwell safely: and this is his name whereby he shall be called, THE LORD OUR RIGHTEOUSNESS.

- ❖ **Jeremiah 46:27** But fear not thou, O my servant Jacob, and be not dismayed, O Israel: for, behold, I will save thee from afar off, and thy seed from the land of their captivity; and Jacob shall return, and be in rest and at ease, and none shall make him afraid.

- **Zechariah 8:13** And it shall come to pass, that as ye were a curse among the heathen, O house of Judah, and house of Israel; so will I save you, and ye shall be a blessing: fear not, but let your hands be strong.

- **Matthew 15:24** But he answered and said, I am not sent but unto the lost sheep of the house of Israel.

- **Luke 1:68-70** 68 Blessed [be] the Lord God of Israel; for he hath visited and redeemed his people, 69 And hath raised up an horn of salvation for us in the house of his servant David; 70 As he spake by the mouth of his holy prophets, which have been since the world began

- **Leviticus 26:17** And I will set my face against you, and ye shall be slain before your enemies: they that hate you shall reign over you; and ye shall flee when none pursueth you.

- **Acts 5:31** Him hath God exalted with his right hand to be a Prince and a Saviour, for to give repentance to Israel, and forgiveness of sins.

- **Romans 9:27** Esaias also crieth concerning Israel, Though the number of the children of Israel be as the sand of the sea, a remnant shall be saved

- **Romans 11:26** And so all Israel shall be saved: as it is written, There shall come out of Sion the Deliverer, and shall turn away ungodliness from Jacob

WORLD

- **Isaiah 45:17** But Israel shall be saved in the LORD with an everlasting salvation: ye shall not be ashamed nor confounded world without end.

❖ **John.18:20** Jesus answered him, I spake openly to the world; I ever taught in the synagogue, and in the temple, whither the Jews always resort; and in secret have I said nothing.

❖ **John12:19** The Pharisees therefore said among themselves, Perceive ye how ye prevail nothing? behold, the world is gone after him.

❖ **2 Esdras 6:59** If the world now be made for our sakes, why do we not possess an inheritance with the world? how long shall this endure?

❖ **John 17:9** I pray for them: I pray not for the world, but for them which thou hast given me; for they are thine.

❖ **1 John 2:15** Love not the world, neither the things that are in the world. If any man love the world, the love of the Father is not in him.

❖ **James 4:4** Ye adulterers and adulteresses, know ye not that the friendship of the world is enmity with God? whosoever therefore will be a friend of the world is the enemy of God.

WHOSOEVER

❖ **Acts.2:21-22 21** And it shall come to pass, [that] whosoever shall call on the name of the Lord shall be saved. 22 Ye men of Israel, hear these words; Jesus of Nazareth, a man approved of God among you by miracles and wonders and signs, which God did by him in the midst of you, as ye yourselves also know

❖ **Joel.2:32** And it shall come to pass, that whosoever shall call on the name of the LORD shall be delivered: for in mount Zion and in Jerusalem shall be deliverance, as the LORD hath said, and in the remnant whom the LORD shall call.

❖ **Acts.13:26** Men and brethren, children of the stock of Abraham, and whosoever among you feareth God, to you is the word of this salvation sent.

He Foreknew

❖ **Amos 3:1** Hear this word that the LORD hath spoken against you, O children of Israel, against the whole family which I brought up from the land of Egypt, saying 2 You only have I known of all the families of the earth: therefore I will punish you for all your iniquities.

❖ **Romans 11:1-2** 1 I say then, Hath God cast away his people? God forbid. For I also am an Israelite, of the seed of Abraham, [of] the tribe of Benjamin. 2 God hath not cast away his people which he foreknew. Wot ye not what the scripture saith of Elias? how he maketh intercession to God against Israel, saying,

❖ **Romans 8:29** For whom he did foreknow, he also did predestinate to be conformed to the image of his Son, that he might be the firstborn among many brethren.

ELECT

❖ **Isaiah 45:4** For Jacob my servant's sake, and Israel mine elect, I have even called thee by thy name: I have surnamed thee, though thou hast not known me.

❖ **Sirach 47:22** But the Lord will never leave off his mercy, neither shall any of his works perish, neither will he abolish the posterity of his elect, and the seed of him that loveth him he will not take away: wherefore he gave a remnant unto Jacob, and out of him a root unto David.

❖ **Matthew 24:31** And he shall send his angels with a great sound of a trumpet, and they shall gather together his elect from the four winds, from one end of heaven to the other.

❖ **Luke 18:7** And shall not God avenge his own elect, which cry day and night unto him, though he bear long with them?

❖ **Romans 8:33** Who shall lay any thing to the charge of God's elect? It is God that justifieth.

CHOSEN

❖ **Deuteronomy 7:6** For thou art an holy people unto the LORD thy God: the LORD thy God hath chosen thee to be a special people unto himself, above all people that are upon the face of the earth.

❖ **Isiah 41:8** But thou, Israel, art my servant, Jacob whom I have chosen, the seed of Abraham my friend.

❖ **Isiah 43:10** Ye are my witnesses, saith the LORD, and my servant whom I have chosen: that ye may know and believe me, and understand that I am he: before me there was no God formed, neither shall there be after me.

❖ **Isiah 44:1-2** 1Yet now hear, O Jacob my servant; and Israel, whom I have chosen: 2Thus saith the LORD that made thee, and formed thee from the womb, which will help thee; Fear not, O Jacob, my servant; and thou, Jesurun, whom I have chosen.

ISLAM created in 622 AD

❖ **Deuteronomy 28:64** And the LORD shall scatter thee among all people, from the one end of the earth even unto the other; and there thou shalt serve other gods, which neither thou nor thy fathers have known, even wood and stone.

❖ **Deuteronomy 32:17** They sacrificed unto devils, not to God; to gods whom they knew not, to new gods that came newly up, whom your fathers feared not.

❖ **Jeremiah 3:2** Lift up thine eyes unto the high places, and see where thou hast not been lien with. In the ways hast thou sat for them, as the Arabian in the wilderness; and thou hast polluted the land with thy whoredoms and with thy wickedness.

❖ **Leviticus 26:1** Ye shall make you no idols nor graven image, neither rear you up a standing image, neither shall ye set up any image of stone in your land, to bow down unto it: for I am the LORD your God.

❖ **Jeremiah 2:27** Saying to a stock, Thou art my father; and to a stone, Thou hast brought me forth: for they have turned their back unto me, and not their face: but in the time of their trouble they will say, Arise, and save us.

❖ **Psalms 83:1-6 (A Song or Psalm of Asaph.)** Keep not thou silence, O God: hold not thy peace, and be not still, O God. 2For, lo, thine enemies make a tumult: and they that hate thee have lifted up the head. 3They have taken crafty counsel against thy people, and consulted against thy hidden ones. 4They have said, Come, and let us cut them off from being a nation; that the name of Israel may be no more in remembrance. 5For they have consulted together with one consent: they are confederate against thee: 6The tabernacles of Edom, and the Ishmaelites; of Moab, and the Hagarenes;

IMMACULATE CONCEPTION LIE

❖ **Matthew 1:16** And Jacob begat Joseph the husband of Mary, of whom was born Jesus, who is called Christ.

❖ **John 1:45** Philip findeth Nathanael, and saith unto him, We have found him, of whom Moses in the law, and the prophets, did write, Jesus of Nazareth, the son of Joseph.

❖ **Matthew 13:55- 56** 55 Is not this the carpenter's son? is not his mother called Mary? and his brethren, James, and Joses, and Simon, and Judas? 56 And his sisters, are they not all with us? Whence then hath this man all these things?

❖ **Luke 2:48** And when they saw him, they were amazed: and his mother said unto him, Son, why hast thou thus dealt with us? behold, thy father and I have sought thee sorrowing.

❖ **Hebrews 2:16-18** 16 For verily he took not on [him the nature of] angels; but he took on [him] the seed of Abraham. 17 Wherefore in all things it behoved him to be made like unto [his] brethren, that he might be a merciful and faithful high priest in things [pertaining] to God, to make reconciliation for the sins of the people.18 For in that he himself hath suffered being tempted, he is able to succour them that are tempted.

❖ **Wisdom of Solomon 7:1-6** I myself also am a mortal man, like to all, and the offspring of him that was first made of the earth, 2 And in my mother's womb was fashioned to be flesh in the time of ten months, being compacted in blood, of the seed of man, and the pleasure that came with sleep.

30

3 And when I was born, I drew in the common air, and fell upon the earth, which is of like nature, and the first voice which I uttered was crying, as all others do. 4 I was nursed in swaddling clothes, and that with cares. 5 For there is no king that had any other beginning of birth. 6 For all men have one entrance into life, and the like going out.

❖ **1 John 4:2** Hereby know ye the Spirit of God: Every spirit that confesseth that Jesus Christ is come in the flesh is of God

❖ **Acts 2:30** Therefore being a prophet, and knowing that God had sworn with an oath to him, that of the fruit of his loins, according to the flesh, he would raise up Christ to sit on his throne

❖ **Leviticus 15:16-18** 16 And if any man's seed of copulation go out from him, then he shall wash all his flesh in water, and be unclean until the even. 17 And every garment, and every skin, whereon is the seed of copulation, shall be washed with water, and be unclean until the even. 18 The woman also with whom man shall lie [with] seed of copulation, they shall [both] bathe [themselves] in water, and be unclean until the even.

❖ **Romans 1:3** Concerning his Son Jesus Christ our Lord, which was made of the seed of David according to the flesh.

❖ **2 Samuel 7:12- 14** 12 And when thy days be fulfilled, and thou shalt sleep with thy fathers, I will set up thy seed after thee, which shall proceed out of thy bowels, and I will establish his kingdom. 13 He shall build an house for my name, and I will stablish the throne of his kingdom for ever. 14 I will be his father, and he shall be my son. If he commit iniquity, I will chasten him with the rod of men, and with the stripes of the children of men

- ❖ **Psalms 132:10-11** 10 For thy servant David's sake turn not away the face of thine anointed. 11 The LORD hath sworn [in] truth unto David; he will not turn from it; Of the fruit of thy body will I set upon thy throne.

- ❖ **Matthew 1:18 (Before they came together)** Now the birth of Jesus Christ was on this wise: When as his mother Mary was espoused to Joseph, before they came together, she was found with child of the Holy Ghost.

- ❖ **Tobit 8:18-20** 18 Then Raguel bade his servants to fill the grave. 19 And he kept the wedding feast fourteen days. 20 For before the days of the marriage were finished, Raguel had said unto him by an oath, that he should not depart till the fourteen days of the marriage were expired

- ❖ **John2:1-2** 1 And the third day there was a marriage in Cana of Galilee; and the mother of Jesus was there 2 And both Jesus was called, and his disciples, to the marriage.

- ❖ **Tobit 7:13- 14** 13Then he called his daughter Sara, and she came to her father, and he took her by the hand, and gave her to be wife to Tobias, saying, Behold, take her after the law of Moses, and lead her away to thy father. And he blessed them; 14And called Edna his wife, and took paper, and did write an instrument of covenants, and sealed it.

- ❖ **Judges 15:1** (Chamber) But it came to pass within a while after, in the time of wheat harvest, that Samson visited his wife with a kid; and he said, I will go in to my wife into the chamber. But her father would not suffer him to go in.

- ❖ **Tobit 6:13** (marriage chamber) Then the young man answered the angel, I have heard, brother Azarias that this maid hath been given to seven men, who all died in the marriage chamber.

❖ **Deuteronomy 22:15-17** (tokens of virginity) 15 Then shall the father of the damsel, and her mother, take and bring forth [the tokens of] the damsel's virginity unto the elders of the city in the gate: 16 And the damsel's father shall say unto the elders, I gave my daughter unto this man to wife, and he hateth her; 17 And, lo, he hath given occasions of speech [against her], saying, I found not thy daughter a maid; and yet these [are the tokens of] my daughter's virginity. And they shall spread the cloth before the elders of the city.

MARRIAGE

❖ **Hebrews 13:4** Marriage is honourable in all, and the bed undefiled: but whoremongers and adulterers God will judge.

❖ **Exodus 22:16** And if a man entice a maid that is not betrothed, and lie with her, he shall surely endow her to be his wife.

❖ **Tobit 7:13- 14** (Papers) 13Then he called his daughter Sara, and she came to her father, and he took her by the hand, and gave her to be wife to Tobias, saying, Behold, take her after the law of Moses, and lead her away to thy father. And he blessed them; 14And called Edna his wife, and took paper, and did write an instrument of covenants, and sealed it.

❖ **Sirach 25:1** In three things I was beautified, and stood up beautiful both before God and men: the unity of brethren, the love of neighbours, a man and a wife that agree together.

❖ **Ecclesiasticus 42:7** Deliver all things in number and weight; and put all in writing that thou givest out, or receivest in.

❖ **Tobit 8:5-9** (age together) 5 Then began Tobias to say, Blessed art thou, O God of our fathers, and blessed is thy holy and glorious name for ever; let the heavens bless thee, and all thy creatures. 6 Thou madest Adam, and gavest him Eve his wife for an helper and stay: of them came mankind: thou hast said, It is not good that man should be alone; let us make unto him an aid like unto himself. 7 And now, O Lord, I take not this my sister for lust but uprightly: therefore mercifully ordain that we may become aged together. 8 And she said with him, Amen. 9 So they slept both that night. And Raguel arose, and went and made a grave

❖ **Ecclesiasticus 6:7** (prove) If thou wouldest get a friend, prove him first and be not hasty to credit him.

❖ **Matthew 19:5** live together And said, For this cause shall a man leave father and mother, and shall cleave to his wife: and they twain shall be one flesh?

❖ **Ephesians 5:22-25-33** 22 Wives, submit yourselves unto your own husbands, as unto the Lord. 23 For the husband is the head of the wife, even as Christ is the head of the church: and he is the saviour of the body. 24 Therefore as the church is subject unto Christ, so let the wives be to their own husbands in every thing. 25Husbands, love your wives, even as Christ also loved the church, and gave himself for it; 33 Nevertheless let every one of you in particular so love his wife even as himself; and the wife see that she reverence her husband.

❖ **Colossians 3:18-19** 18 Wives, submit yourselves unto your own husbands, as it is fit in the Lord. 19 Husbands, love [your] wives, and be not bitter against them.

❖ **1 Corinthians 7:1-2, 10-16** 1 Now concerning the things whereof ye wrote unto me: It is good for a man not to touch a woman. 2 Nevertheless, to avoid fornication, let every man have his own wife, and let every woman have her own husband. 10 And unto the married I command, yet not I, but the Lord, Let not the wife depart from her husband: 11But and if she depart, let her remain unmarried, or be reconciled to her husband: and let not the husband put away his wife. 12 But to the rest speak I, not the Lord: If any brother hath a wife that believeth not, and she be pleased to dwell with him, let him not put her away. 13 And the woman which hath an husband that believeth not, and if he be pleased to dwell with her, let her not leave him. 14 For the unbelieving husband is sanctified by the wife, and the unbelieving wife is sanctified by the husband: else were your children unclean; but now are they holy. 15 But if the unbelieving depart, let him depart. A brother or a sister is not under bondage in such cases: but God hath called us to peace. 16 For what knowest thou, O wife, whether thou shalt save thy husband? or how knowest thou, O man, whether thou shalt save thy wife?

❖ **1 Peter 3:1-7** 1 Likewise, ye wives, [be] in subjection to your own husbands; that, if any obey not the word, they also may without the word be won by the conversation of the wives; 2 While they behold your chaste conversation [coupled] with fear. 3 Whose adorning let it not be that outward [adorning] of plaiting the hair, and of wearing of gold, or of putting on of apparel; 4 But [let it be] the hidden man of the heart, in that which is not corruptible, [even the ornament] of a meek and quiet spirit, which is in the sight of God of great price. 5 For after this manner in the old time the holy women also, who trusted in God, adorned themselves, being in subjection unto their own husbands: 6 Even as Sara obeyed Abraham, calling him lord: whose daughters ye are, as long as ye do well, and are not afraid with any amazement. 7 Likewise, ye husbands, dwell with [them] according to knowledge, giving honour unto the wife, as unto the weaker vessel, and as being heirs together of the grace of life; that your prayers be not hindered.

DIVORCE

* **Deuteronomy 24:1-4** 1 When a man hath taken a wife, and married her, and it come to pass that she find no favour in his eyes, because he hath found some uncleanness in her: then let him write her a bill of divorcement, and give it in her hand, and send her out of his house. 2 And when she is departed out of his house, she may go and be another man's wife. 3 And if the latter husband hate her, and write her a bill of divorcement, and giveth it in her hand, and sendeth her out of his house; or if the latter husband die, which took her to be his wife; 4 Her former husband, which sent her away, may not take her again to be his wife, after that she is defiled; for that is abomination before the LORD: and thou shalt not cause the land to sin, which the LORD thy God giveth thee for an inheritance.

* **Jeremiah 3:1** They say, If a man put away his wife, and she go from him, and become another man's, shall he return unto her again? shall not that land be greatly polluted? but thou hast played the harlot with many lovers; yet return again to me, saith the LORD.

* **Matthew 19:9** And I say unto you, Whosoever shall put away his wife, except it be for fornication, and shall marry another, committeth adultery: and whoso marrieth her which is put away doth commit adultery.

* **Mark 10:12** And if a woman shall put away her husband, and be married to another, she committeth adultery.

❖ **1 Corinthians 7:39** The wife is bound by the law as long as her husband liveth; but if her husband be dead, she is at liberty to be married to whom she will; only in the Lord.

❖ **Romans 7:2-3** 2 For the woman which hath an husband is bound by the law to [her] husband so long as he liveth; but if the husband be dead, she is loosed from the law of [her] husband. 3 So then if, while [her] husband liveth, she be married to another man, she shall be called an adulteress: but if her husband be dead, she is free from that law; so that she is no adulteress, though she be married to another man.

❖ **1 Corinthians 7:15** But if the unbelieving depart, let him depart. A brother or a sister is not under bondage in such cases: but God hath called us to peace.

❖ **Ecclesiasticus 25:26** If she go not as thou wouldest have her, cut her off from thy flesh, and give her a bill of divorce, and let her go.

❖ **1 Corinthians 7:3-5** 3 Let the husband render unto the wife due benevolence: and likewise also the wife unto the husband. 4 The wife hath not power of her own body, but the husband: and likewise also the husband hath not power of his own body, but the wife. 5 Defraud ye not one the other, except it be with consent for a time, that ye may give yourselves to fasting and prayer; and come together again, that Satan tempt you not for your incontinency.

GOOD WIFE

❖ **Tobit 8:6-8** 6 Thou madest Adam, and gavest him Eve his wife for an helper and stay: of them came mankind: thou hast said, It is not good that man should be alone; let us make unto him an aid like unto himself. 7 And now, O Lord, I take not this my sister for lust but uprightly: therefore mercifully ordain that we may become aged together. 8 And she said with him, Amen.

❖ **Sirach 25:1 (agree)** In three things I was beautified, and stood up beautiful both before God and men: the unity of brethren, the love of neighbours, a man and a wife that agree together.

❖ **Sirach 26:1-3** Blessed is the man that hath a virtuous wife, for the number of his days shall be double. 2 A virtuous woman rejoiceth her husband, and he shall fulfil the years of his life in peace. 3 A good wife is a good portion, which shall be given in the portion of them that fear the Lord.

❖ **Sirach 26:14 (quiet wife)** A silent and loving woman is a gift of the Lord; and there is nothing so much worth as a mind well instructed.

EVIL WOMAN

❖ **Ecclesiastes 7:26** And I find more bitter than death the woman, whose heart is snares and nets, and her hands as bands: whoso pleaseth God shall escape from her

❖ **1 Esdras 4:26- 27** 26 Yea, many there be that have run out of their wits for women, and become servants for their sakes. 27 Many also have perished, have erred, and sinned, for women.

❖ **Proverbs 7:10-12** 10 And, behold, there met him a woman with the attire of an harlot, and subtil of heart. 11 (She is loud and stubborn; her feet abide not in her house: 12 Now is she without, now in the streets and lieth in wait at every corner.)

❖ **Ezekiel 16:44-46** 44 Behold, every one that useth proverbs shall use this proverb against thee, saying, As is the mother, so is her daughter. 45 Thou art thy mother's daughter that lotheth her husband and her children; and thou art the sister of thy sisters, which lothed their husbands and their children: your mother was an Hittite, and your father an Amorite. 46 And thine elder sister is Samaria, she and her daughters that dwell at thy left hand: and thy younger sister, that dwelleth at thy right hand.

❖ **Sirach 25:23-25** 23 A wicked woman abateth the courage, maketh an heavy countenance and a wounded heart: a woman that will not comfort her husband in distress maketh weak hands and feeble knees. 24 Of the woman came the beginning of sin, and through her we all die. 25 Give the water no passage; neither a wicked woman liberty to gad abroad.

❖ **Sirach 26:7 (scorpion)** An evil wife is a yoke shaken to and fro: he that hath hold of her is as though he held a scorpion.

❖ **Sirach 26:23-27** 23 A wicked woman is given as a portion to a wicked man: but a godly woman is given to him that feareth the Lord. 24 A dishonest woman contemneth shame: but an honest woman will reverence her husband. 25 A shameless woman shall be counted as a dog; but she that is shamefaced will fear the Lord. 26 A woman that honoureth her husband shall be judged wise of all; but she that dishonoureth him in her pride shall be counted ungodly of all. 27 A loud crying woman and a scold shall be sought out to drive away the enemies.

❖ **Ecclesiasticus 42:10 (baby in fathers house)** In her virginity, lest she should be defiled and gotten with child in her father's house; and having an husband, lest she should misbehave herself; and when she is married, lest she should be barren.

ORDER OF WOMEN

❖ **Genesis 3:16** Unto the woman he said, I will greatly multiply thy sorrow and thy conception; in sorrow thou shalt bring forth children; and thy desire shall be to thy husband, and he shall rule over thee.

❖ **1 Corinthians 11:3-9** 9 But I would have you know, that the head of every man is Christ; and the head of the woman is the man; and the head of Christ is God. 4 Every man praying or prophesying, having his head covered, dishonoureth his head, 5 But every woman that prayeth or prophesieth with her head uncovered dishounoureth her head: for that is even all one as if she were shaven. 6 For if the woman be not covered, let her also be shorn: but if it be a shame for a woman to be shorn or shaven, let her be covered. 7 For a man indeed ought not to cover his head, forasmuch as he is the image and glory of God: but the woman is the glory of the man. 8 For the man is not of the woman; but the woman of the man. 9 Neither was the man created for the woman; but the woman of the man.

❖ **Numbers 30:3-8** 3 If a woman also vow a vow unto the Lord, and bind herself by a bond, being in her father's house in her youth; 4 And her father hear her vow, and her bond wherewith she hath bound her soul, and her father shall hold his peace at her: then all her vows shall stand, and every bond wherewith she hath bound her soul shall stand. 5 But if her father disallow her in the day that he heareth; not any of her vows, or of her bonds wherewith she hath bound her soul, shall stand: and the Lord shall forgive her, because her father disallowed her. 6 And if she had at all an husband, when she vowed, or uttered ought out of her lips, wherewith she bound her soul; 7 And her husband heard it, and held his peace at her in the day that he heard it: then her vows shall stand, and her bonds wherewith she bound her soul shall stand. 8 But if her husband disallowed her on the day that he heard it; then he shall make her vow which she vowed, and that which she uttered with her lips, wherewith she bound her soul, of none effect: and the Lord shall forgive her.

❖ **1 Timothy 2:9-15** 9 In like manner also, that women adorn themselves in modest apparel, with shamefacedness and sobriety; not with broided hair, or gold, or pearls, or costly array; 10 But (which becometh women professing godliness) with good works. 11 Let the woman learn in silence with all subjection. 12 But I suffer not a woman to teach, nor to usurp authority over the man, but to be in silence. 13 For Adam was first formed, then Eve. 14 And Adam was not deceived, but the woman being deceived was in the transgression. 15 Notwithstanding she shall be saved in childbearing, if they continue in faith and charity and holiness with sobriety.

❖ **1 Corinthians 14:34- 35** 34 Let your women keep silence in the churches: for it is not permitted unto them to speak: but they are commanded to be under obedience, as also saith the law. 35 And if they will learn any thing, let them ask their husbands at home: for it is a shame for women to speak in the church.

❖ **Titus 2:3-5** 3 The aged women likewise, that they be in behaviour as becometh holiness, not false accusers, not given to much wine, teachers of good things; 4 That they may teach the young women to be sober, to love their husbands, to love their children, 5 To be discreet, chaste, keepers at home, good, obedient to their own husbands, that the word of God be not blasphemed.

MARRIAGE SEX LAWS

❖ **Hebrews 13:4** Marriage is honourable in all, and the bed undefiled: but whoremongers and adulterers God will judge.

❖ **1 Corinthians 7:2-5** 2 Nevertheless, to avoid fornication, let every man have his own wife, and let every woman have her own husband. 3 Let the husband render unto the wife due benevolence: and likewise also the wife unto the husband. 4 The wife hath not power of her own body, but the husband: and likewise also the husband hath not power of his own body, but the wife. 5 Defraud ye not one the other, except it be with consent for a time, that ye may give yourselves to fasting and prayer: and come together again, that Satan tempt you not for your incontinency.

❖ **Leviticus 15:16-18 (Seed)** 16 And if any man's seed of copulation go out from him, then he shall wash all his flesh in water, and be unclean until the even. 17 And every garment, and every skin, whereon is the seed of copulation, shall be washed with water, and be unclean until the even. 18 The woman also with whom man shall lie with seed of copulation, they shall both bathe themselves in water, and be unclean until the even.

❖ **Leviticus 15:19-24 (menstrual)** 15 And if a woman have an issue, and her issue in her flesh be blood, she shall be put apart seven days: and whosoever toucheth her shall be unclean until the even. 20 And every thing that she lieth upon in her separation shall be unclean: every thing also that she sitteth upon shall be unclean. 21 And whosoever thoucheth her bed shall wash his clothes, and bathe himself in water, and be unclean until the even. 22 And whosoever toucheth any thing that she sat upon shall wash his clothes, and bathe himself in water, and be unclean until the even. 23 And if it be on her bed, or on any thing whereon she sitteth, when he toucheth it, he shall be unclean until the even. 24 And if any man lie with her at all, and her flowers be upon him, he shall be unclean seven days; and all the bed whereon he lieth shall be unclean.

❖ **Leviticus 20:18 (sex on menstrual)** And if a man shall lie with a woman having her sickness, and shall uncover her nakedness; he hath discovered her fountain, and she hath uncovered the fountain of her blood: and both of them shall be cut off from among their people.

❖ **Leviticus 12 (male/female baby)** 1 And the LORD spake unto Moses, saying, 2 Speak unto the children of Israel, saying, If a woman have conceived seed, and born a man child: then she shall be unclean seven days; according to the days of the separation for her infirmity shall she be unclean. 3 And in the eighth day the flesh of his foreskin shall be circumcised. 4 And she shall then continue in the blood of her purifying three and thirty days; she shall touch no hallowed thing, nor come into the sanctuary, until the days of her purifying be fulfilled. 5 But if she bear a maid child, then she shall be unclean two weeks, as in her separation: and she shall continue in the blood of her purifying threescore and six days. 6 And when the days of her purifying are fulfilled, for a son, or for a daughter, she shall bring a lamb of the first year for a burnt offering, and a young pigeon, or a turtledove, for a sin offering, unto the door of the tabernacle of the congregation, unto the priest: 7 Who shall offer it before the LORD, and make an atonement for her; and she shall be cleansed from the issue of her blood. This is the law for her that hath born a male or a female. 8 And if she be not able to bring a lamb, then she shall bring two turtles, or two young pigeons; the one for the burnt offering, and the other for a sin offering: and the priest shall make an atonement for her, and she shall be clean.

❖ **Leviticus 18:7-23 (unlawful sex)** 7 The nakedness of thy father, or the nakedness of thy mother, shalt thou not uncover: she [is] thy mother; thou shalt not uncover her nakedness. 8 The nakedness of thy father's wife shalt thou not uncover: it [is] thy father's nakedness. 9 The nakedness of thy sister, the daughter of thy father, or daughter of thy mother, [whether she be] born at home, or born abroad, [even] their nakedness thou shalt not uncover. 10 The nakedness of thy son's daughter, or of thy daughter's daughter, [even] their nakedness thou shalt not uncover: for theirs [is] thine own nakedness. 11 The nakedness of thy father's wife's daughter, begotten of thy father, she [is] thy sister, thou shalt not uncover her nakedness. 12 Thou shalt not uncover the nakedness of thy father's sister: she [is] thy father's near kinswoman. 13 Thou shalt not uncover the nakedness of thy mother's sister: for she [is] thy mother's near kinswoman. 14 Thou shalt not uncover the nakedness of thy father's brother, thou shalt not approach to his wife: she [is] thine aunt. 15 Thou shalt not uncover the nakedness of thy daughter in law: she [is] thy son's wife; thou shalt not uncover her nakedness. 16 Thou shalt not uncover the nakedness of thy brother's wife: it [is] thy brother's nakedness. 17 Thou shalt not uncover the nakedness of a woman and her daughter, neither shalt thou take her son's daughter, or her daughter's daughter, to uncover her nakedness; [for] they [are] her near kinswomen: it [is] wickedness. 18 Neither shalt thou take a wife to her sister, to vex [her], to uncover her nakedness, beside the other in her life [time]. 19 Also thou shalt not approach unto a woman to uncover her nakedness, as long as she is put apart for her uncleanness. 20 Moreover thou shalt not lie carnally with thy neighbour's wife, to defile thyself with her. 21 And thou shalt not let any of thy seed pass through [the fire] to Molech, neither shalt thou profane the name of thy God: I [am] the LORD. 22 Thou shalt not lie with mankind, as with womankind: it [is] abomination. 23 Neither shalt thou lie with any beast to defile thyself therewith: neither shall any woman stand before a beast to lie down thereto: it [is] confusion.

CHRISTMAS

❖ **Jeremiah 10:1-5** 1 Hear ye the word which the LORD speaketh unto you, O house of Israel: 2 Thus saith the LORD, Learn not the way of the heathen, and be not dismayed at the signs of heaven; for the heathen are dismayed at them. 3 For the customs of the people [are] vain: for [one] cutteth a tree out of the forest, the work of the hands of the workman, with the axe. 4 They deck it with silver and with gold; they fasten it with nails and with hammers, that it move not. 5 They [are] upright as the palm tree, but speak not: they must needs be borne, because they cannot go. Be not afraid of them; for they cannot do evil, neither also [is it] in them to do good.

❖ **Revelation 11:10** And they that dwell upon the earth shall rejoice over them, and make merry, and shall send gifts one to another; because these two prophets tormented them that dwelt on the earth.

❖ **Wisdom of Solomon 14:16** Thus in process of time an ungodly custom grown strong was kept as a law, and graven images were worshipped by the commandments of kings.

❖ **Colossians 2:8** Beware les any man spoil you through philosophy and vain deceit, after the tradition of men, after the rudiments of the world, and not after Christ.

❖ **Titus 1:14** Not giving heed to Jewish fables, and commandments of men, that turn from the truth.

❖ **2 Peter 1:16** For we have not followed cunningly devised fables, when we made known unto you the power and coming of our Lord Jesus Christ, but were eyewitnesses of his majesty.

STUDY

- ❖ **2 Timothy 2:15** Study to shew thyself approved unto God, a workman that needeth not to be ashamed, rightly dividing the word of truth.

- ❖ **Proverbs 15:28** The heart of the righteous studieth to answer: but the mouth of the wicked poureth out evil things.

- ❖ **1 Peter 3:15** But sanctify the Lord God in you hearts: and be ready always to give an answer to every man that asketh you a reason of the hope that is in you with meekness and fear

- ❖ **Ecclesiasticus 6:32** My son, if thou wilt, thou shalt be taught: and if thou wilt apply thy mind, thou shalt be prudent.

- ❖ **Jude 20** But ye, beloved, building up your selves on your most holy faith, praying in the Holy Ghost

STUDY THE WHOLE BIBLE

- ❖ **Matthew 4:4** But he answered and said, It is written, Man shall not live by bread alone, but by every word that proceedeth out of the mouth of God.

- ❖ **2 Timothy 3:16** All scripture is given by inspiration of God, and is profitable for doctrine, for reproof, for correction, for instruction in righteousness

- ❖ **Hebrews 10:7** Then said I, Lo, I come (in the volume of the book it is written of me,) to do thy will, O God.

❖ **Matthew 13:52** Then said he unto them, Therefore every scribe which in instructed unto the kingdom of heaven is like unto a man that is an householder, which bringeth forth out of his treasure things new and old.

THE BIBLE IS ONLY FOR ISRAEL

❖ **Psalms 147:19-20** 19 He sheweth his word unto Jacob, his statutes and his judgments unto Israel. 20 He hath not dealt so with any nation: and as for his judments, they have not known them. Praise ye the Lord.

❖ **Baruch 3:36** He hath found out all the way of knowledge, and hath given it unto Jacob his servant, and to Israel his beloved.

❖ **Romans 3:1-2** 1 What advantage then hath the Jew? Or what profit is there of circumcision? 2 Much every way: chiefly, because that unto them were committed the oracles of God.

HOW TO READ THE BIBLE

❖ **Isaiah 28:9-10** 9 Whom shall he teach knowledge? And whom shall he make to understand doctrine? Them that are weaned from the milk, and drawn from the breasts. 10 For precept must be upon precept, precept upon precept; line upon line, line upon line; here a little, and there a little

❖ **1 Peter 1:20-21** 20 Who verily was foreordained before the foundation of the world, but was manifest in these last times for you, 21 Who by him do believe in God, that raised him up from the dead, and gave him glory; that your faith and hope might be in God.

❖ **Sirach 6:37** Let thy mind be upon the ordinances of the Lord and meditate continually in his commandments: he shall establish thine heart, and give thee wisdom at thine owns desire.

❖ **Acts 8:30-31** 30 And Philip ran thither to him, and heard him read the prophet Esaias and said, Understandest thou what thou readest? 31 And he said, How can I, except some man should guide me? And he desired Philip that he would come up and sit with him.

OPPRESSION

❖ **Deuteronomy 28:29-33** 29 And thou shalt grope at noonday, as the blind gropeth in darkness, and thou shalt not prosper in thy ways: and thou shalt be only oppressed and spoiled evermore, and no man shall save thee. 30 Thou shalt betroth a wife, and another man shall lie with her: thou shalt build an house, and thou shalt not dwell therein: Thou shalt plant a vineyard, and shalt not gather the grapes thereof. 31 Thine ox shall be slain before thine eyes, and thou shalt not eat thereof: tine ass shall be violently taken away from before thy face, and shall not be restored to thee: thy sheep shall be given unto thine enemies, and thou shalt have none to rescue them. 32 Thy sons and thy daughters shall be given unto another people, and thine eyes shall look, and fail with longing for them all the day long: and there shall be no might in thine hand. 33 The fruit of thy land, and all thy labours, shall a nation which thou knowest not eat up; and thou shalt be only oppressed and crushed alway

❖ **Ecclesiastes 7:7** Surely oppression maketh a wise man mad; and a gift destroyeth the heart.

❖ **Proverbs 3:31** Envy thou not the oppressor, and choose none of his ways.

❖ **Jeremiah 50:33** Thus saith the Lord of hosts; The children of Israel and the children of Judah were oppressed

together: and all that took them captives held them fast;
they refused to let them go.

❖ **Sirach 35:13** He will not accept any person against a poor
man, but will hear the prayer of the oppressed.

ISRAELITES CALLED HEATHENS

❖ **Ezekiel 20:32** And that which cometh into your mind shall
not be at all, that ye say, We will be as the heathen, as the
families of the countries, to serve wood and stone.

❖ **Ezekiel 25:8** Thus saith the Lord God: Because that Moab
and Seir do say, Behold, the house of Judah is like unto all
the heathen

❖ **Galatians 3:8** And the scripture, forseeing that God would
justify the heathen through faith, preached before the
gospel unto Abraham, saying In thee shall all nations be
blessed.

ISRAELITES CALLED GENTILES

2 Maccabees 6:8-9 8 Moreover there went out a decree to the
neighbour cities of the heathen, by the suggestion of Ptolemee,
against the Jews, that they should observe the same fashions,
and be partakers of their sacrifices 9 And whoso would not
conform themselves to the manners of the Gentiles should be put
to death. Then might a man have seen the present misery.

John 7:35 Then said the Jews among themselves, Whither will he
go, that we shall not find him? Will he go unto the dispersed
among the Gentiles, and teach the Gentiles?

Romans 9:24-26 24 Even us, whom he hath called, not of the Jews
only, but also of the Gentiles? 25 As he saith also in Osee, I will
call them my people, which were not my people; and her beloved,

which was not beloved. 26 And it shall come to pass, that in the place where it was said unto them, Ye are not my people; there shall they be called the children of the living God.

Hosea 1:10-11 10 Yet the number of the children of Israel shall be as of the sand of the sea, which cannot be measured nor numbered; and it shall come to pass, that in the place where it was said unto them, Ye are the sons of the living God. 11 Then shall the children of Judah and the children of Israel be gathered together, and appoint themselves one head, and they shall come up out of the land: for great shall be the day of Jezreel.

Matthew 4:15 The land of Zabulon, and the land of Nephthalim, by the way of the sea, beyond Jordan, Galilee of the Gentiles

1 Corinthians 12:2 Ye know that ye were Gentiles, carried away unto these dumb idols, even as ye were led.

Isaiah 11:10-12 10 And in that day there shall be a root of Jesse, which shall stand for an ensign of the people; to it shall the Gentiles seek; and his rest shall be glorious. 11 And it shall come to pass in that day, that the Lord shall set his hand again the second time to recover the remnant of his people, which shall be left, from Assyria, and from Egypt, and from Pathros, and from Cush, and from Elam, and from Shinar, and from Hamath, and from the islands of the sea. 12 And he shall set up an ensign for the nations, and shall assemble the outcasts of Israel, and gather together the dispersed of Judah from the four corners of the earth.

REAL GENTILE NATIONS

1 Esdras 8:69 The nation of Israel, the princes, the priests and Levites, have not put away from them the strange people of the land, nor the pollutions of the Gentiles to wit, of the Canaanites, Hittites, Pheresites, Jebusites, and the Moabites, Egyptians, and Edomites.

Genesis 10:5 By these were the isles of the Gentiles divided in their lands; every one after his tongue, after their families, in their nations.

Jeremiah 46:1-2 The word of the Lord which came to Jeremiah the prophet against the Gentiles; 2 Against Egypt, against the army of Pharaohnecho king of Egypt, which was by the river Euphrates in Carchemish, which Nebuchadrezzar king of Babylon smote in the fourth year of Jehoiakim the son of Josiah king of Judah.

Isaiah 60:11-12 11 Therefore thy gates shall be open continually; they shall not be shut day nor night; that men may bring unto thee the forces of the Gentiles, and that their kings may be brought. 12 For the nation and kingdom that will not serve thee shall perish; yea, those nations shall be utterly wasted.

Isaiah 61:9 And their seed shall be known among the Gentiles, and their offspring among the people: all that se them shall acknowledge them, that they are the seed which the Lord hath blessed.

STRANGERS NATIONS

Leviticus 25:44-47 (law) 44 Both thy bondmen, and thy bondmaids, which thou shalt have, shall be of the heathen that are round about you; of them shall ye buy bondmen and bondmaids. 45 Moreover of the children of the strangers that do sojourn among you, of them shall ye buy, and of their families that are with you, which they begat in your land: and they shall be your possession. 46 And ye shall take them as an inheritance for your children after you, to inherit them for a possession; they shall be your bondmen for ever; but over your brethren the children of Israel, ye shall not rule one over another with rigour. 47 And if a sojourner or stranger wax rich by thee, and thy brother that dwelleth by him wax poor, and sell himself unto the stranger or sojourner by thee, or to the stock of the stranger's family

Deuteronomy 28:43-44 43 The stranger that is within thee shall get up above thee very high; and thou shalt come down very low. 44 He shall lend to thee, and thou shalt not lend to him: he shall be the head, and thou shalt be the tail.

Jeremiah 5:19 And it shall come to pass, when ye shall say, Wherefore doeth the Lord our God all these things unto us? Then shalt thou answer them, Like as ye have forsaken me, and served strange gods in your land, so shall ye serve strangers in a land that is not yours.

Nehemiah 9:2 And the seed of Israel separated themselves from all strangers, and stood and confessed their sins, and the iniquities of their fathers

Isaiah 14:1-3 3 For the Lord will have mercy on Jacob, and will yet choose Israel, and set them in their own land: and the strangers shall be joined with them, and they shall cleave to the house of Jacob. 2 And the people shall take them, and bring them to their place: and the house of Israel shall possess them in the land of the Lord for servants and handmaids: and they shall take them captives, whose captives they were; and they shall rule over their oppressors. 3 And it shall come to pass in the day that the Lord shall give thee rest from they sorrow, and from thy fear, and from the hard bondage wherein thou wast made to serve

Isaiah 60:10 And the sons of strangers shall build up thy walls, and their kings shall minister unto thee: for in my wrath I smote thee, but in my favour have I had mercy on thee.

Isaiah 61:5 And strangers shall stand and feed your flocks, and the sons of the alien shall be your plowmen and your vinedressers.

Joel 3:17 So shall ye know that I am the Lord your God dwelling in Zion, my holy mountain: then shall Jerusalem be holy, and there shall no strangers pass through her any more.

Jeremiah 30:8 For it shall come to pass in that day, saith the Lord of hosts, that I will break his yoke from off my neck, and will burst thy bonds, and strangers shall no more serve themselves of him

Isaiah 1:7 Your country is desolate, your cities are burned with fire: your land, strangers devour it in you presence, and it is desolate, as overthrown by strangers.

Isaiah 2:6 Therefore thou has forsaken thy people the house of Jacob, because they be replenished from the east, and are soothsayers like the Philistines, and they please themselves in the children of strangers.

ISRAEL CALLED STRANGERS

Obadiah v.12 But thou shouldest not have looked on the day of thy brother in the day that he became a stranger; neither shouldest thou have rejoiced over the children of Judah in the day of their destruction; neither shouldest thou have spoken proudly in the day of distress.

Ephesians 2:12,19 12 That at that time ye were without Christ, being aliens from the commonwealth of Israel, and strangers from the covenants of promise, having no hope, and without God in the world 19 Now therefore ye are no more strangers and foreigners, but fellow-citizens with the saints, and of the household of God

1Peters 1:1 Perter, an apostle of Jesus Christ, to the strangers scattered throughout Pontus, Galatia, Cappadocia, Asia, and Bithynia

INTERRACIAL MARRIAGE

Deuteronomy 7:3 Neither shalt thou make marriages with them; thy daughter thou shalt not give unto his son, nor his daughter shalt thou take unto thy son.

Joshua 23:12-13 12 Else if ye do in any wise go back, and cleave unto the remnant of these nations, even these that remain among you, and shall make marriages with them, and go in unto them, and they to you; 13 Know for a certainty that the Lord your God will no more drive out any of these nations from before you; but they shall be snares and traps unto you, and scourges in your sides, and thorns in your eyes, until ye perish from off this good land which the Lord your God hath given you.

Nehemiah 13:23-27 23 In those days also saw I Jews that had married wives of Ashdod, of Ammon, and of Moab: 24 And their children spake half in the speech of Ashdod, and could not speak in the Jews' language, but according to the language of each people. 25 And I contended with them, and cursed them, and smote certain of them, and plucked off their hair, and made them swear by God, saying, Ye shall not give your daughters unto their sons, not take their daughters unto your sons, or for yourselves. 26 Did not Solomon king of Israel sin by these things? Yet among many nations was there no king like him, who was beloved of his God, and God made him king over all Israel: nevertheless even him did outlandish women cause to sin. 27 Shall we then hearken unto you to do all this great evil, to transgress against our God in marrying strange wives?

1 Esdras 8:84 Therefore now shall ye not join your daughters unto their sons, neither shall ye take their daughters unto your sons.

Tobit 4:12-13 12 Beware of all whoredom, my son, and chiefly take a wife of the seed of thy fathers, and take not a strange woman to wife, which is not of thy father's tribe: for we are the children of the prophets, Noe, Abraham, Isaac, and Jacob: remember, my son, that our fathers from the beginning, even that

54

they all married wives of their own kindred, and were blessed in their children, and their seed shall inherit the land. 13 Now therefore, my son, love thy brethren, and despise not in thy heart thy brethren, the sons and daughters of thy people, in not taking a wife of them: for in pride is destruction and much trouble, and in lewdness is decay and great want: for lewdness is the mother of famine.

Malachi 2:11-15 11 Judah hath dealt treacherously, and an abomination is committed in Israel and in Jerusalem; for Judah hath profaned the holiness of the Lord which he loved, and hath married the daughter of a strange god. 12 The Lord will cut off the man that doeth this, the master and the scholar, out of the tabernacles of Jacob, and him that offereth an offering unto the Lord of hosts. 13 And this have ye done again, covering the altar of the Lord with tears, with weeping, and with crying out, insomuch that he regardeth not the offering any more, or receiveth it with good will at your hand. 14 Yet ye say, Wherefore? Because the Lord hath been witness between thee and the wife of thy youth, against whom thou hast dealt treacherously; yet is she thy companion, and the wife of thy covenant. 15 And did not he make one? Yet had he residue of the spirit. And wherefore one? That he might seek a godly seed. Therefore take heed to your spirit, and let none deal treacherously against the wife of his youth.

<u>REGENERATION</u>

Ecclesiastes 1:9-11 9 The thing that hath been, it is that which shall be; and that which is done is that which shall be done: and there is no new thing under the sun. 10 Is there any thing whereof it may be said, See this is new? It hath been already of old time, which was before us. 11 There is no remembrance of former things; neither shall there be any remembrance of things that are to come with those that shall come after.

Job 19:25-27 25 For I know that my redeemer liveth, and that he shall stand at the latter day upon the earth: 26 And though after my skin worms destroy this body, yet in my flesh shall I see God: 27 Whom I shall see for myself, and mine eyes shall behold, and not another; though my reins be consumed within me.

Malachi 4:5-6 5 Behold, I will send you Elijah the prophet before the coming of the great and dreadful day of the Lord: 6 And he shall turn the heart of the fathers to the children, and the heart of the children to their fathers, lest I come and smite the earth with a curse.

Matthew 17:11-13 11 And Jesus answered and said unto them, Elias truly shall first come, and restore all things. 12 But I say unto you, That Elias is come already, and they knew him not, but have done unto him whatsoever they listed. Likewise shall also the Son of man suffer of them. 13 Then the disciples understood that he spake unto them of John the Baptist.

Matthew 19:28 And Jesus said unto them, Verily I say unto you, That That ye which have followed me, in the regeneration when the Son of man shall sit in the throne of his glory, ye also shall sit upon twelve thrones, judging the twelve tribes of Israel.

Revelation 10:11 And he said unto me, Thou must prophesy again before many peoples, and nations, and tongues, and kings.

Daniel 12:13 But go thou thy way till the end be: for thou shalt rest, and stand in thy lot at the end of the days.

Numbers 24:17 I shall see him, but not now: I shall behold him, but not nigh: there shall come a Star out of Jacob, and a Sceptre shall rise out of Israel, and shall smite the corners of Moab, and destroy all the children of Sheth.

2 Esdras 1:38-40 38 And now, brother, behold what glory; and see the people that come from the east: 39 Unto whom I will give for leaders, Abraham, Isaac, and Jacob, Oseas, Amos, and Micheas, Joel, Abdias, and Jonas, 40 Nahum, and Abacuc, Sophonias,

Aggeus, Zachary, and Malachy, which is called also an angel of the Lord.

UFO'S ARE CHARIOTS

Ezek.1:4,16,19,21 4 And I looked, and, behold, a whirlwind came out of the north, a great cloud, and a fire infolding itself, and a brightness was about it, and out of the midst thereof as the colour of amber, out of the midst of the fire. 16 The appearance of the wheels and their work was like unto the colour of a beryl: and they four had one likeness: and their appearance and their work was as it were a wheel in the middle of a wheel. 19 And when the living creatures went, the wheels went by them: and when the living creatures were lifted up from the earth, the wheels were lifted up. 21 When those went, these went: and when those stood, these stood: and when those were lifted up from the earth, the wheels were lifted up over against them: for the spirit of the living creature was in the wheels.

Psalms 104:3 Who layeth the beams of his chambers in the waters: who maketh the clouds his chariot: who walketh upon the wings of the wind

Psalms 68:17 The chariots of God are twenty thousand, even thousands of angels: the Lord is among them, as in Sinai, in the holy place.

Isaiah 66:15 For, behold, the Lord will come with fire, and with his chariots like a whirlwind, to render his anger with fury, and his rebuke with flames of fire.

Daniel 7:9 I beheld till the thrones were cast down, and the Ancient of days did sit, whose garments was white as snow, and the hair of his head like the pure wool: his throne was like the fiery flame, and his wheels as burning fire.

Zechariah 5:1-5 1 Then I turned, and lifted up mine eyes, and looked, and behold a flying roll. 2 And he said unto me, What seest thou? And I answered, I see a flying roll; the length thereof is twenty cubits, and the breadth thereof ten cubits. 3 Then said he unto me, This is the curse that goeth forth over the face of the whole earth: for every one that stealeth shall be cut off as on this side according to it; and every one that sweareth shall be cut off as on that side according to it. 4 I will bring it forth, saith the Lord of hosts, and it shall enter into the house of the thief, and into the house of him that sweareth falsely by my name: and it shall remain in the midst of his house, and shall consume it with the timber thereof and the stones thereof. 5 Then the angel that talked with me went forth, and said unto me, Lift up now thine eyes, and see what is this that goeth forth.

SABBATH

Genesis 2:1-2 (made holy) 1 Thus the heavens and the earth were finished, and all the host of them. 2 And on the seventh day God ended his work which he had made: and he rested on the seventh day from all his work which he had made.

Exodus 20:8-11 (no work) 8 Remember the sabbath day, to keep it holy 9 Six days shalt thou labour, and do all thy work: 10 But the seventh day is the sabbath of the Lord thy God: in it thou shalt not do any work, thou nor thy son, nor thy daughter, thy manservant, nor thy maidservant, nor thy cattle, nor thy stranger that is within thy gates: 11 For in six days the Lord made heaven and earth, the sea, and all that in them is, and rested the seventh day: wherefore the Lord blessed the sabbath day, and hallowed it.

Exodus 16:23 (no cooking) And he said unto them, This is that which the Lord hath said, Tomorrow is the rest of the holy sabbath unto the Lord: bake that which ye will bake to day, and seethe that ye will seethe; and that which remaineth over lay up for you to be kept until the morning.

Exodus 35:3 (no fire) Ye shall kindle no fire throughout your habitations unto the sabbath day.

Nehemiah 10:31 (no buying or selling) And if the people of the land bring ware or any victuals on the sabbath day to sell, that we would not buy it of them on the sabbath, or on the holy day: and that we would leave the seventh year, and the exaction of every debt.

Nehemiah 13:15-21 (detail) 15 In those days saw I in Judah some treading wine presses on the sabbath, and bringing in sheaves, and lading asses; as also wine, grapes, and figs, and all manner of burdens, which they brought into Jerusalem on the sabbath day: and I testified against them in the day wherein they sold victuals. 16 There dwelt men of Tyre, also therein, which brought fish, and all manner of ware, and sold on the sabbath unto the children of Judah, and in Jerusalem. 17 Then I contended with the nobles of Judah, and said unto them, What evil thing is this that ye do, and profane the sabbath day? 18 Did not your fathers thus, and did not our God bring all this evil upon us, and upon this city? Yet ye bring more wrath upon Israel by profaning the sabbath 19 And it came to pass, that when the gates of Jerusalem began to be dark before the sabbath, I commanded that the gates should be shut, and charged that they should not be opened till after the sabbath: and some of my servants set I at the gates, that there should no burden be brought in on the sabbath day. 20 So the merchants and sellers of all kind of ware lodged without Jerusalem once or twice. 21 Then I testified against them, and said unto them, Why lodge ye about the wall? If ye do so again, I will lay hands on you. From that time forth came they no more on the sabbath.

DRESS CODE

Isaiah 52:1 Awake, awake; put on thy strength, O Zion; put on thy beautiful garments, O Jerusalem, the holy city: for henceforth there shall no more come into thee the uncircumcised and the unclean.

Numbers 15:38-40 38 Speak unto the children of Israel, and bid them that they make them fringes in the borders of their garments throughout their generations, and that they put upon the finge of the borders a ribband of blue: 39 And it shall be unto you for a fringe, that ye may look upon it, and remember all the commandments of the Lord, and do them; and that ye seek not after your own heart and your own eyes, after which use to go a whoring: 40 That ye may remember, and do all my commandments, and be holy unto your God.

Ezekiel 16:11-14 11 I decked thee also with ornaments, and I put bracelets upon thy hands, and a chain on thy neck. 12 And I put a jewel on thy forehead, and earrings in thine ears, and a beautiful crown upon thine head. 13 Thus wast thou decked with god and silver; and thy raiment was of fine linen, and silk, and broidered work; thou didst eat fine flour, and honey, and oil: and thou wast exceeding beautiful, and thou didst prosper into a kingdom. 14 And thy renown went forth among the heathen of thy beauty: for it was perfect through my comeliness, which I had put upon thee, saith the Lord God.

1 Maccabees 14:9 The ancient men sat all in the streets, communing together of good things, and the young men put on glorious and warlike apparel.

HATRED

Leviticus 19:17 Thou shalt not hate thy brother in thine heart: thou shalt in any wise rebuke thy neighbour, and not suffer sin upon him.

Proverbs 11:12 He that is void of wisdom despiseth his neighbour: but a man of understanding holdeth his peace.

1 John 3:15 Whosoever hateth his brother is a murderer; and ye know that no murderer hath eternal life abiding in him.

1 John 4:20 If a man say, I love God, and hateth his brother, he is a liar; for he that loveth not his brother whom he hath seen, how can he love God whom he hath not seen?

Matthew 5:21-24 21 Ye have heard that it was said by them of old time, Thou shalt not kill; and whosoever shall kill shall be in danger of the judgment: 22 But I say unto you, That whosoever is angry with his brother without a cause shall be in danger of the judgment: and whosoever shall say to his brother, Raca, shall be in danger of the council: but whosoever shall say, Thou fool, shall be in danger of hell fire. 23 Therefore if thou bring thy gift before the altar, and there rememberest that thy brother hath ought against thee; 24 Leave there thy gift before the altar, and go thy way; first be reconciled to thy brother, and then come and offer thy gift.

DESTRUCTION

Isaiah 54:16 Behold, I have created the smith that bloweth the coals in the fire, and that bringeth forth an instrument for his work; and I have created the waster to destroy.

2 Peter 3:10-12 10 But the day of the Lord will come as a thief in the night; in the which the heavens shall pass away with a great noise, and the elements shall melt with fervent heat, the earth also and the works that are therein shall be burned up. 11 Seeing then that all these things shall be dissolved, what manner of persons ought ye to be in all holy conversation and godliness, 12 Looking for and hasting unto the coming of the day of God, wherein the heavens being on fire shall be dissolved, and the elements shall melt with fervent heat?

Zechariah 14:12 And this shall be the plague wherewith the Lord will smite all the people that have fought against Jerusalem; Their flesh shall consume away while they stand upon their feet, and their eyes shall consume away in their holes, and their tongue shall consume away in their mouth.

Isaiah 34:4-6 4 And all the host of heaven shall be dissolved, and the heavens shall be rolled together as a scroll: and all their host shall fall down, as the leaf falleth off from the vine, and as a falling fig from the fig tree. 5 For my sword shall be bathed in heaven: behold, it shall come down upon Idumea, and upon the people of my curse, to judgment. 6 The sword of the Lord is filled with blood, it is made fat with fatness, and with the blood of lambs and goats, with the fat of the kidneys of rams; for the Lord hath a sacrifice in Bozrah, and a great slaughter in the land of Idumea.

Matthew 24:29-31 29 Immediately after the tribulation of those days shall the sun be darkened, and the moon shall not give her light, and the stars shall fall from heaven, and the powers of the heavens shall be shaken: 30 And then shall appear the sign of the Son of man in heaven: and then shall all the tribes of the earth mourn, and they shall see the Son of man coming in the clouds of heaven with power and great glory. 31 And he shall send his angels with a great sound of a trumpet, and they shall gather together his elect from the four winds, from on end of heaven to the other.

2 Thessalonians 1:6-9 6 Seeing it is a righteous thing with God to recompense tribulation to them that trouble you; 7 And to you who are troubled rest with us, when the Lord Jesus shall be revealed from heaven with his mighty angels, 8 In flaming fire taking vengeance on them that know not God, and that obey not the gospel of our Lord Jesus Christ: 9 Who shall be punished with everlasting destruction from the presence of the Lord, and from the glory of his power

Revelation 6:14 And the heaven departed as a scroll when it is rolled together; and every mountain and island were moved out of their places.

Psalms 91:5-8 5 Thou shalt not be afraid for the terror by night; nor for the arrow that flieth by day; 6 Nor for the pestilence that walketh in darkness; nor for the destruction that wasteth at noonday. 7 A thousand shall fall at thy side, and ten thousand at thy right hand; but it shall not come nigh thee. 8 Only with thine eyes shalt thou behold and see the reward of the wicked. 9 Because thou hast made the Lord, which is my refuge, even the most High, thy habitation

2 Esdras 13:29-38 29 Behold, the days come, when the most High will begin to deliver them that are upon the earth. 30 And he shall come to the astonishment of them that dwell on the earth. 31 And one shall undertake to fight against another, one city against another, one place against another, one people against another, and one realm against another. 32 And the time shall be when these things shall come to pass, and the signs shall happen which I shewed thee before, and then shall my Son be declared, whom thou sawest as a man ascending. 33 And when all the people hear his voice, every man shall in their own land leave the battle they have one against another. 34 And an innumerable multitude shall be gathered together, as thou sawest them, willing to come, and to overcome him by fighting. 35 But he shall stand upon the top of the mount Sion. 36 And Sion shall come, and shall be shewed to all men, being prepared and builded, like as thou sawest the hill graven without hands. 37 And this my Son shall rebuke the wicked inventions of those nations, which for their wicked life are fallen into the tempest; 38 And shall lay before them their evil thoughts, and the torments wherewith they shall begin to be tormented, which are like unto a flame: and he shall destroy them without labour by the law which is like unto me.

NATIONS IN CAPTIVITY

Numbers 24:17-18 17 I shall see him, but not now: I shall behold him, but not nigh: there shall come a Star out of Jacob, and a Sceptre shall rise out of Israel, and shall smite the corners of Moab, and destroy all the children of Sheth. 18 And Edom shall be a possession, Seir also shall be a possession for his enemies; and Israel shall do valiantly.

Psalms 149 1 Praise ye the LORD. Sing unto the LORD a new song, and his praise in the congregation of saints. 2 Let Israel rejoice in him that made him: let the children of Zion be joyful in their King. 3 Let them praise his name in the dance: let them sing praises unto him with the timbrel and harp. 4 For the LORD taketh pleasure in his people: he will beautify the meek with salvation. 5 Let the saints be joyful in glory: let them sing aloud upon their beds. 6 Let the high praises of God be in their mouth, and a twoedged sword in their hand; 7 To execute vengeance upon the heathen, and punishments upon the people; 8 To bind their kings with chains, and their nobles with fetters of iron; 9 To execute upon them the judgment written: this honour have all his saints. Praise ye the LORD.

Isaiah 14:1-3 For the Lord will have mercy on Jacob, and will yet choose Israel, and set them in their own land: and the strangers shall be joined with them, and they shall cleave to the house of Jacob. 2 And the people shall take them, and bring them to their place: and the house of Israel shall possess them in the land of the Lord for servants and handmaids: and they shall take them captives, whose captives they were; and they shall rule over their oppressors. And it shall come to pass in the day that the Lord shall give thee rest from thy sorrow, and from thy fear and from the hard bondage wherein thou wast made to serve

Isaiah 60:10-14 10 And the sons of strangers shall build up thy walls, and their kings shall minister unto thee: for in my wrath I smote thee, but in my favour have I had mercy on thee. 11 Therefore thy gates shall be open continually; they shall not be shut day nor night: that men may bring unto thee the forces of the Gentiles, and that their kings may be brought, 12 For the nation and kingdom that will not serve thee shall perish; yea, those nations shall be utterly wasted, 13 The glory of Lebanon shall come unto thee, the fir tree, the pine tree, and the box together, to beautify the place of my sanctuary; and I will make the place of my feet glorious. 14 The sons also of them that afflicted thee shall come bending unto thee; and all they that despised thee shall bow themselves down at the soles of thy feet; and they shall call thee, The city of the Lord, The Zion of the Holy One of Israel.

Isaiah 49:23-26 23 And kings shall be thy nursing fathers, and their queens thy nursing mothers; they shall bow down to thee with their face toward the earth, and lick up the dust of thy feet; and thou shalt know that I am the Lord: for they shall not be ashamed that wait for me. 24 Shall the prey be taken from the mighty, or the lawful captive delivered? 25 But thus saith the Lord, Even the captives of the mighty shall be taken away, and the prey of the terrible shall be delivered: for I will contend with him that contendeth with thee, and I will save thy children. 26 And I will feed them that oppress thee with their own flesh; and they shall be drunken with their own blood, as with sweet wine: and all flesh shall know that I the Lord am thy Saviour and thy Redeemer, the mighty One of Jacob.

Isaiah45:14 Thus saith the Lord, The labour of Egypt, and merchandise of Ethiopia and of the Sabeans, men of stature, shall come over unto thee, and they shall be thine: they shall come after thee; in chains they shall come over, and they shall fall down unto thee, they shall make supplication unto thee, saying, Surely God is in thee; and there is none else, there is no God

Jeremiah 30:16 Therefore all they that devour thee shall be devoured; and all thine adversaries, every one of them, shall go into captivity; and they that spoil thee shall be a spoil, and all that prey upon thee will I give for a prey.

Amos 9:11-12 11 In that day will I raise up the tabernacle of David that is fallen, and close up the breaches thereof; and I will raise up his ruins and I will build it as in the days of old: 12 That they may possess the remnant of Edom, and of all the heathen, which are called by my name, saith the Lord that doeth this.

Revelation 13:10 He that leadeth into captivity shall go into captivity: he that killeth with the sword must be killed with the sword. Here is the patience and the faith of the saints.

BAPTISM

Isaiah 1:16 Wash you, make you clean; put away the evil of your doings from before mine eyes; cease to do devil

Jeremiah 2:22 For though thou wash thee with nitre, and take thee much soap, yet thine iniquity is marked before me, saith the Lord God.

Matthew 3:6 And were baptized of him in Jordan, confessing their sins.

John 4:1-2 When therefore the Lord knew how the Pharisees had heard that Jesus made and baptized more disciples than John, (Though Jesus himself baptized not, but his disciples)

John 15:3 Now ye are clean through the word which I have spoken unto you.

1 Peter 3:21 The like figure whereunto even baptism doth also now save us (not the putting away of the filth of the flesh, but the answer of a good conscience toward God,) by the resurrection of Jesus Christ.

Solutions

Now we know our oppression is because of the Nations in power the Bible speaks of .

While in captivity our forefathers seen the end and prayed for us in the future because we would have no power
And be taken advantage of
They told us how to get out of being killed in the streets being at the bottom among all the Nations.
they would have compassion on us ..if we do this ...no marching involved

1 Kings 8:46 If they sin against thee, (for there is no man that sinneth not,) and thou be angry with them, and deliver them to the enemy, so that they carry them away captives unto the land of the enemy, far or near;
1 Kings 8:47 Yet if they shall bethink themselves in the land whither they were carried captives, and repent, and make supplication unto thee in the land of them that carried them captives, saying, We have sinned, and have done perversely, we have committed wickedness;
1 Kings 8:48 And so return unto thee with all their heart, and with all their soul, in the land of their enemies, which led them away captive, and pray unto thee toward their land, which thou gavest unto their fathers, the city which thou hast chosen, and the house which I have built for thy name:
1 Kings 8:49 Then hear thou their prayer and their supplication in heaven thy dwelling place, and maintain their cause,
1 Kings 8:50 And forgive thy people that have sinned against thee, and all their transgressions wherein they have transgressed against thee, and give them compassion before them who carried them captive, that they may have compassion on them

High Holy Days

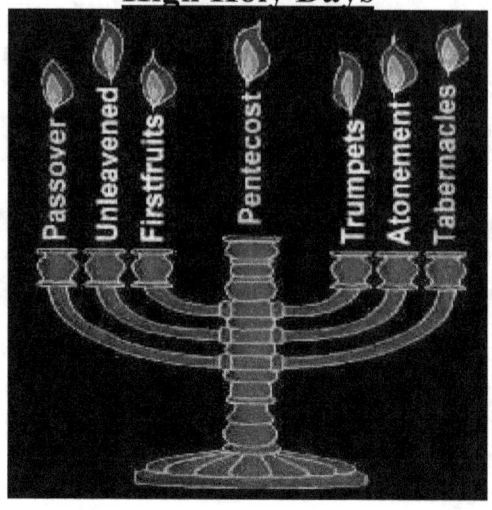

Sabbath (Leviticus 23:3)
Passover/Feast of Unleavened Bread (Lev. 23:5-8)
Feast of First Fruits/ Pentecost (Leviticus 23:15)
Blowing of Trumpets (Leviticus 23:24)
Day of Atonement (Leviticus 23:27)
Feast of Tabernacles (Leviticus 23:34)
New Moons (2 Chronicles 8:13)

The Lord commanded His followers to keep certain High Holy days to honor Him (Leviticus 23:1-44). These High Holy days were kept by many faithful servants of the Lord throughout history, including the prophet Moses, the High Priest Aaron, King David, King Solomon, the prophet Elijah, the son of God Jesus Christ, and the Apostle Paul. However, the origins of most holidays celebrated by Christians today, such as Easter, December 25, Halloween, Valentine's Day, New Year's Day, Thanksgiving Day, and other festivals, are pagan in origin and far different from what the early disciples of Christ followed. While we associate them with Christianity, they were acquired from religions of the Romans, Greeks, and other groups who worshipped both the sun and a multitude of Gods.

The Sabbath is the first commandment given to Adam in the Garden of Eden and the most important of all days. Jesus Christ calls himself Lord of the Sabbath. He emphatically states, "Think not that I am come to destroy the law, or the prophets: I am not come to destroy, but to fulfil" (Matthew 5:17). The Sabbath is one of the Ten Commandments [4th Commandment] given to Moses, written by the finger of God (Deuteronomy 9:10). It is to be kept on the seventh day of every week (sundown Friday to sundown Saturday). God firmly instructs us in Exodus 20:10-11, "The seventh day is the Sabbath of the LORD thy God: in it thou shalt not do any work, thou, nor thy son, nor thy daughter, thy manservant, nor thy maidservant, nor thy cattle, nor thy stranger that is within thy gates: For in six days the LORD made heaven and earth, the sea, and all that in them is, and rested the seventh day: wherefore the LORD blessed the Sabbath day, and hallowed it." This statement is a clear message from God, and He does not change His mind. Many people today use the seventh day for shopping, working, and even partying.

Some people teach that Hebrews 4 defines the seventh-day Sabbath commandment as a shadow-type law pointing forward to a spiritual rest in Christ. They view the Sabbath in the same way the Old Testament sacrifices pointed forward to Christ's atoning death on the cross. They teach that once we have found "spiritual rest" in Christ, we no longer need to observe the Sabbath day. However, the Bible says "…let God be true, but every man a liar; as it is written" Romans 3:4. This means no man or woman, even if they are a pastor, a scholar, a minister, or priest can change the law. We must follow what is written, how it is written, not listen to people's reasoning about why we don't need to follow it anymore. Did the Messiah shop, work, or party on the Sabbath? No! "Now Jesus came to Nazareth, where he had been brought up, and went into the synagogue on the Sabbath day, as was his custom. He stood up to read" (Luke 4:16). The disciples and the Apostle Paul kept the Sabbath as well, even after Christ's ascension. "And the next Sabbath day came almost the whole city together to hear the word of God" (Acts 13:44).

To move away from pagan traditions and follow the Hebraic ways of Christ, we simply must read the law (First five books of the Bible) and learn the acceptable practices. The first thing we must do to keep the Sabbath is rejoice in it because it is a hallowed day, given to us by the Most High God (Exodus 20:11). While we should work hard in our duties six days of the week, we are to use the Sabbath as a day to recover and rest. We should not worry about worldly things such as paying bills, making appointments, or any other type of work, but rather spend time in prayer, meditation, and reading of scriptures. We must be firm with jobs and employers about our 'religious' practices and the need to have off on the Sabbath (Exodus 35:2). Keeping the Sabbath day holy is a commandment from God. Even if we have to pass up one job, the Most High will bless us with an even greater opportunity if we keep His commandment. We are not to buy and sell, shop, or money change on the Sabbath either (Nehemiah 13:15-22). We should either stay within our homes or congregate in holy convocation (Exodus 16:29, Leviticus 23:3). Cooking is forbidden as well (Exodus 16:22-23). This means we should prepare our foods on the sixth day of the week 'Friday' and eat foods that do not need to be cooked on the Sabbath (sandwiches, salads, dips, crackers, etc). We are also not to do our own pleasures but must do the will of Yah. Things such as hanging out, watching worldly movies, and casual sexual relations are not proper practices on the Sabbath. The marriage bed is undefiled and sexual relations can be kept among husband and wives on the Sabbath (Hebrews 13:4).

Today, some people who know the pagan origins of holidays continue to practice them, rationalizing that the family bonding, traditions, and happy times during the holidays make them worth it. However, the Bible says differently. Colossians 2:8 emphatically states, "Beware lest any man spoil you through philosophy and vain deceit, after the tradition of men, after the rudiments of the world, and not after Christ." To follow Christ means we must live and worship the way He did, not after the pagan ways created by men. Some argue that we should celebrate His birthday to honor Him. This again goes against the ways of Christ. It was never part of the traditions of the Messiah to celebrate birthdays. Nowhere in

70

the Bible did anyone celebrate the birthday of Christ or any other important prophets. They worshipped the Creator, not the created. Birthday celebrations are mentioned in the Bible on two separate occasions. In each case, something terrible occurred. The first account is in Genesis. Pharaoh, the Egyptian king, celebrated his birthday by executing his chief baker (Gen. 40:20-23).

In the second account, King Herod reluctantly ordered the beheading of John the Baptist (Matt. 14:3-11). December 25 has never actually been documented as the actual birth of Jesus Christ anyway. Celebrating December 25 came from pagan sun worshipers who celebrated four days after the Winter Solstice as a celebration of lights with the worst of winter behind and increased daylight. Gift exchange began in the 1800s.

Santa Clause represents Thor

Pagan Christmas Tree

The Lord speaks directly against false holidays when He says, "I hate, I despise your feast days, and I will not smell in your solemn assemblies" (Amos 5:21). The Lord even talks against the use of Christmas trees in Jeremiah chapter 10:2-4, "Thus saith the LORD, Learn not the way of the heathen, and be not dismayed at the signs of heaven; for the heathen are dismayed at them. For the customs of the people are vain: for one cutteth a tree out of the forest, the work of the hands of the workman, with the axe. They deck it with silver and with gold; they fasten it with nails and with hammers, that it move not." The Lord will be coming back with vengeance on those who are disobedient. Remember, "Not every one that saith unto me, Lord, Lord, shall enter into the kingdom of heaven; but he that doeth the will of my Father which is in heaven" (Matthew 7:21). We can celebrate pagan holidays to make our families happy, or we can celebrate the Lord's High Holy days to please Him.

Easter is another pagan celebration intertwined with Jesus the Messiah. Bunnies are from the pagan festival of Eostre, a great northern goddess whose symbol was a rabbit or hare. Exchange of eggs is an ancient custom, celebrated by many cultures to represent a fertility goddess. The Passover was the true way to celebrate the sacrifice of the Messiah giving His life for the atonement of our sins.

The Bible says, "Purge out therefore the old leaven, that ye may be a new lump, as ye are unleavened. For even Christ our Passover is sacrificed for us" (1 Corinthians 5:7). The Last Supper was a Passover meal the Messiah celebrated with His twelve disciples. "And He [Jesus Christ] said unto them, With desire I have desired to eat this Passover with you before I suffer" (Luke 22:15). When we celebrate the Passover, we not only honor a commandment of Yah (Leviticus 23:5), we also honor the heritage of Christ by keeping the same festival He kept. The Passover takes place on the first full moon after the spring equinox and is commemorated with seven days of holy convocation and feasting. The foods include unleavened bread, bitter herbs, vegetables, and any other lawful foods of our choice (never pork or shellfish). The foods cannot contain leaven such as most breads and pastries. Besides the physical foods, we must also have the spiritual food, the words of the Messiah. He is our Passover lamb. "Man shall not live by bread alone, but by every word that proceeds out of the mouth of God" (Matthew 4:4). Scripture should be read during the feast. It is a time to celebrate, dance, and rejoice in it!

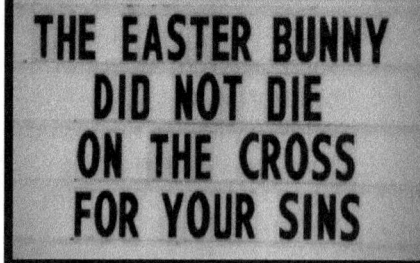

The convening of the Council of Nicaea in AD 325 was orchestrated by the Roman Emperor Caesar Flavius Constantine. During this assembly, Emperor Constantine presided over a gathering of church bishops and leaders, aiming to establish a unified understanding of God within Christianity. The Council overwhelmingly affirmed Jesus Christ's divinity and delineated the relationship between the Father and the Son as "of one substance," solidifying the concept of the Trinity with the Father, Son, and Holy Spirit as three co-equal and co-eternal Persons. However, this doctrinal stance diverges from the biblical teachings and the principles espoused by Jesus Christ. In contrast to pagan Roman practices, the Hebrew faith emphasizes the oneness of God, as expressed in passages like "Hear, O Israel: The LORD our God is one LORD" (Deuteronomy 6:4). Jesus himself emphasized obedience to God's commandments and asserted his alignment with the Father's will rather than a self-determined purpose. The notion of the Trinity, as well as the observance of Easter, marked significant departures from the Yahweh-centered traditions, steering people toward human-influenced practices. It's important to note that the Council of Nicaea did not determine the inclusion of books in the Bible; Hebrew priests, prophets, and disciples safeguarded scripture, including Apocryphal books, to preserve the traditions aligned with the Heavenly Father.

www.ingramcontent.com/pod-product-compliance
Lightning Source LLC
Chambersburg PA
CBHW070936120626
46546CB00004B/1431